Scattering Light

The Quantum Entanglement
of
William G. Gray
&
Alan Richardson

Dedicated to…

The staff of Newport Hospital on the Isle of Wight and the crew of the island's Helicopter Ambulance, who ferried me like the nearly-lost soul I was to Southampton Hospital, where I also received superb care.

My wife Margaret, who went through personal hells during all this, and my daughters Zoe, Kirsty, Jade and Lara, plus Beau and baby Cassidy, who dropped everything and streamed down to support us both.

Of course I must especially thank the very subjects of this book, William G. Gray and Roberta F. Gray who were always kind to me and taught me many things in what seems like the Ancient of Days, but in this case was actually 40 years ago.

And also: Rebsie Fairholm, Daniel Staniforth and Basil Wilby; Suzanne Ruthven, Sean Martin, Kerri Sharp and Judith Page – they know why, and how much I owe them all.

I don't have a website, but for anyone interested, many of my other books can be found on Amazon. I think I've still got a somewhat wearied 'Alan Richardson' page there. Be warned that I'm not the Alan Richardson who does cookery books, and I'm definitely *not* the Alan Richardson who is – apparently – a famous American theologian. Look for the weird titles and you might find me.

'Scattering of light gives rise to many spectacular phenomena. It is caused when light rays deviate from their original path upon striking an obstacle like dust or water vapours...'

Or an obstacle like me.

Or an obstacle like thee...

'Alan, if you're really determined to write books, then make sure that each one is original, or don't bloody bother…'
William G. Gray c.1969

'Bill, I've done my best with each one…'
Alan Richardson 23/4/23

Table of Contents

1	Introduction/Explanation	5
2	Second Tranche of 'Quantum' Letters	7
3	Disentangling	180
4	'Porno from Crowley's Magical Diary	182

Cover photograph was taken by A.C. Highfield, who Bill Gray mentions in the Second Tranche and who has always played an odd part in all of this oddness without it being obvious to anyone at the time. That marvellous picture of the Moon was captured during a moment of High Strangeness that he had, and it seemed appropriate to include it here. Andy does not have a website but you can access his superb work on Instagram via *andyhighfieldphotography* and also contact him on Facebook.

Introduction/Explanation

In the late Summer of 2022 I had a major heart attack while on a walking holiday in the Isle of Wight. I was taken in the helicopter ambulance to the mainland where I received superb care at Southampton General Hospital, under the (for me) flawless aegis of our oft-scorned NHS. Since then, while recuperating, I spent some time doing what everyone does after being faced with the sudden knowledge that they are probably not immortal: sorting out my documents.

At the bottom of my wardrobe was a large box marked, tongue-in-cheekly, *Letters from the Magi*, packed with letters I'd received from my teens onward when a Stamped Addressed Envelope, sent to an author via their publishers, was often a sure-fire way of getting a response. There was also another hefty one called *Letters from Dolores*, that I remember as always funny, rude and startling on many levels. And there was a third (to which I paid no immediate attention), marked *Letters from W.G. Gray*. I put that to one side.

It was only recently that I decided to peer into the latter. There, on the top, was what I must now call the 'First Tranche' from Gray to me between the years of 17 and 21, when he banished me from his door, as he did almost everyone. The lovely indie Skylight Press published these as *Letters of Light* in 2015.

Below these however, was what I must now call the 'Second Tranche', if only because I rather like that word. These began in 1983 and carried on spasmodically up to his death in 1992. Although I haven't read through them yet, I believe that somewhere in that stack will be the last letter he ever wrote. There was a very different tone to these. After all, I was a very different person, and no longer the awestruck youth playing Private Pike to his Captain Mainwaring. You might have to Google that one...

If there are unfamiliar references in what follows, I can only refer you to....

Me, MySelf and Dion Fortune.
Letters of Light.
The Inner Realms of Christine Hartley.
The Old Sod, by me and Marcus Claridge.

You see I am still recuperating, still get tired and somewhat frightened, and don't want to create an all-explaining, footnote-heavy text. In this era a quick search of the Web will do the trick if you need these details.

Throughout the writing, I've had an under-thrumming of great sadness. Re-reading his letters, I see them filled with spiritual certainty, brilliance, inspiration and hope, but I know how it all ends, and so I became a bitter-sweet aspect of Merlin. You know the tale: Merlin sees a young couple dancing and singing with joy after their marriage, and he bursts into tears, because he knows that they will soon die horribly of the plague; and then he sees an old shrivelled man, clad in rags, dying of cold and hunger and he bursts out laughing, because he knows there is a crock of gold just beneath him. Merlin, it could be argued, should have done something about both. Yet while I was writing this, Bill managed to fulfil a childhood dream of mine and turned me into a Time Lord: for me, his future had already happened. I was powerless to help.

So without further ado, let me get the letters of the Second Tranche out of the box, read them for the first time in 40 years, and reply to them a day at the time, though I'm already surprised at how many there are. I might have to prune.

I will also keep some of Bill's formatting and the unjustified lines to partially re-create what *all* letters looked like in those days when done on the old typewriters.

(Remember those? Some of them now sell for more than a pc, though I can't imagine anyone idiotic enough to buy one.)

Wm. G. Gray
14. Bennington St.
Cheltenham
Glos. GL50 4ED

Telephone

(0242) 24129

18 April 1983

Dear Alan,

Nice to hear from you after all this time. Last I remember you sent me a very sad note implying that you were all washed up and I'd never hear from you again. You may not remember it, but you did. And here you turn up again all bouncy with a string of writings to your name, Good for you.

Sorry, but I can't help you at all, but I would if I could. I've never even heard of Seymour, let alone met him, and I couldn't care less about the guy anyhow. I don't know Christine Hartley either, except know she was involved with the Inner Light before I was. God preserve me from living to the dreadful age of 86, and God help her for being it.

As I see it, we need less digging up of past figures and more to help with the appalling present. That is if anything can help. I should think it might be an idea to shoot every politician in the world in every country on the same day. That might only postpone the Day of Doom, but at least it might give us more time to learn how to live with each other instead of simply wondering how to survive. Or IF survival would be worth while.

At the moment I've got four books in the pipeline with Weisers, the first two reputedly coming out in June now, and the others by dribs and drabs. Just about the last I'm likely to write in this incarnation, though Carr Collins keeps nagging at me to do a book about Tarot, which I think is utterly unnecessary since so many quite interesting ones have been done already.

My only concern with Arthur mythology is its Grail connections and implications, which is the thesis behind this new series in the bag. Far far older than any Arthur of course, So far, we have a Temple going in Johannesburg, another forthcoming in Brazil, (Masonic-Rosicrucian connection there) but absolutely nothing at all in Britain that I know of. But I'm not much in touch these days. About one visit to South Africa every year, a. few letters here and there with relatively unimportant people, - and that's about my ageing life this moment. I don't keep a personal circle going any longer, can't be bothered with the hassle and hou-ha .

Very occasionally I do an article for the Lamp of Thoth, (Chris Brays mag from the Sorcerers Apprentice) Its getting a bit crummy by now, but it was good at first. that's about the way all these "Occult magazines" end up. Pity the good old "Occult Review" packed up. It got a bit stuffy, but at least all its contributors were reputable people with something sound to say. It wouldn't pay to-day. No sex and violence in it. Nothing slurpy and sensational.

Thinking about re-incarnation, I've been following up a curious track on the rebirth of someone I knew a few years back who committed suicide, and I have good grounds for suspicion has reappeared as the son of a couple I know. Anyway there are a hell of a lot of indications all pointing in the same direction. can't be more certain until the child begins to talk in about another three or four years. Its a longish and most involved story, but its moral seems to be that suicide isn't a good idea as a general whole at all, and only shoots one back again to learn the lessons one refused to face previously.

Back in 37-8, most psychics were backing the "No War" line, and it kicked the shit out of them when it _did_ break loose. Actually a. good kick up the arse was what most of them needed with all their "Masters", Gurus, and "" barking up every wrong tree in the Zodiac. I well remember all the crawl-downs and excuses that followed, plus most of the scuttlings from London at great speed. Occult records in those days were not exactly impressive.

Old Israel Regardie I believe is working away on a. new presentation of Golden Dawn personalities based on a _huge_ collection papers supplied by Gerald Yorke. I can't imagine why any modern person wants to bother with them. They were a classical example of how NOT to run an Occult Association, and that's about all. What the hell does it matter who screwed who long after all parties are dead?? Or who buggered the Great Beast in 1897??? About the only thing that really matters is how are we to make sure that there will even _be_ the next century in human history, and can <u>anything</u> spiritual prevent the destruction of humanity by its own hand? If so, we need to know what that may he and bring it to bear as quickly as possible,

This time there will be NO "Saviours" or Redeemer-Figures appearing at all. When I was your age, all the hopes of the "Occult world" (probably no more than a few old ladies) were pinned on the Great and Mysterious World Teacher who was going to appear and save us from ourselves. Anyone believing something like that now must be either plain nuts or just clinging to a pathetic fantasy. Either we save ourselves or get blasted to buggery, We need <u>time</u> most of all. Plus the determination to use it properly.

Now I come to think of it, wasn't Christine Hartley connected vaguely with Ithell Colquhoun?

Curious in the Occult, how often some character lives a relatively quiet life, then a few years only after their deaths, and all writers want to start jumping on the bandwagon of a long and dreary series of books about the defunct personage. A few years back it was Crowley, then Blake. It'll get round to Dion Fortune presently, and she'll be credited with all sorts of things she didn't do, debited with all activities she wouldn't have done - or couldn't, romanced about and generally distorted until there are no more Sales to be got out of the wretched woman's psychic corpse. I don't doubt presently somebody will have a posthumous go at poor old Bill Butler. For all I know Dolores Nowicki is doing just that right now,

By the way, Bobby wants to send you her best regards, I wish you luck and hope you get a relatively honest publisher. Weisers do pay up in the end, but not without a struggle. Just as well I'm not writing for the sake of money, and thank God I'm nearly at the end of this depressing incarnation. Last lap now, and I hope I don't get shunted beck here for a long long time, Some younger chap asked if I would care to come back as his son later on, and was a bit put out at my reply. He meant it well enough too.

Good luck with your work. Sorry I can't help, but I would have done if I could have done, even though you are right in assuming I wouldn't have had a lot of sympathy with the idea. For Gods sake don't write anything about me after I'm dead, or there'll be trouble for you, By the way, have you ever considered if this dead chap would have wanted you to write him up? Surely he has the right to some consideration in the matter. DF herself would have strongly objected to it, even though she knew quite well she ran the risk, Why should anyone be public property after their deaths to writers who wouldn't have passed the time of day with them when alive???

Sincerely,

Garden Office
West Wiltshire
27th February, 2023

Hello Bill – and the lovely Bobbie!

It has been almost exactly 40 years since I received and read that letter. I am now the same age as you were when you wrote it. It feels very odd to me, opening a small window in Time, and hearing you again. I'm reminded that you wrote exactly as you spoke, rhythms and all.

Are we having something of a Quantum Entanglement here? Not that I really understand much about the Quantum thingies, and can only (probably wrongly) parrot: *Everything that can happen **does** happen; You **can** be in two places at the same time; there is no such thing as Time.*

So here am I on a bitterly cold morning in the small office in our long and narrow garden, probably on the same line of longitude as you in your study in Cheltenham, some fifty miles or so to the north and forty years in my past. I look out at the birds and the mangy Mystery Cat from god knows where and I see there is a whole world out there, Bill, living its own life without reference to our dead-alive existences.

Your voice came through so clearly I wonder if there's a part of you, typing away on 18 April 1983, that might be aware of my presence? If so, you wouldn't recognise me now, as you didn't recognise the young, vigorous spirit of your own Dad when he came back to you in your teens. I'm a very different person now, and quite horrified by what a shit I was for most of my life, and some might argue still am.

Did you – do you? - hear me?

Several things leap from your letter. I note that you 'don't keep a personal circle going'. We're very much alike in that respect, though in my case it's because I'm not very good doing the 'friend thing' these days, and perhaps never was. You rail against this present urge that people have in 1983 to do biographies via the digging up of 'psychic corpses' (I like that term!), and warn: 'don't write anything about me after I'm dead, or there'll be trouble for you', but under this Second Tranche of your letters I have the original MS of your own autobiography. Maybe having me in the back of your mind nudged you into doing it.

Reincarnation? And the possible rebirth of someone you knew a few years back who committed suicide? That was Roy Bowers, who used the Coven name, if that's the right term, of Robert Cochrane. You had a lot to do with him and his group, the short-lived Clan of Tubal Cain. While admitting that he certainly had Power (he healed a long-standing ailment of yours) you also felt he was a bit of a phoney, although a charismatic one.

I think all of us in this odd business of Magic have a degree of phoneyness – myself in particular. Or do I mean a mad sort of self-belief that enables us to leap the various abysses we encounter? One of the members of that coven was Evan John Jones, and he spoke very highly of you, while sharing your reservations about Cochrane. In an article in a now defunct and forgotten (by me) magazine he wrote: 'If one who claims to be a Witch can perform the tasks of Witchcraft, i.e. summon the spirits and they come, can divine with rod, fingers and birds. If they can also claim the right to the omens and have them; have the power to call, heal and curse and above all, can tell the maze and cross the Lethe, then you have a witch.'

Personally I would apply that to magicians too. So many of them just make noises. You Bill, had power. You were a Mars and Geburah figure, for good and ill. Bobbie seemed to me to be of Jupiter and Chesed. With my limited experience of marriages at the time, I assumed that that you balanced well.

Your letter is a sort of necronomicon, a book of dead names...

You mentioned 'Old Regardie'. Francis Israel Regardie was only a couple of years older than you! I remember that you fell out when he objected to you calling him 'Frank' instead of Francis, which he said was something of an honorific given to him by one of his female admirers.

And Gerald Yorke! I know Yorke lived near you in Gloucestershire and gave you a very rude hand-written poem by Crowley that you said looked as if he'd wiped his arse on it. After sniffing it, Yorke said he probably did. And weren't you and Yorke involved with Military Intelligence at some point in the War? A lot of people in the magical groups were. It was the deva-like Murry Hope, who lived not far from you in Charlton Kings, who told me that, and who *also* claimed to have worked for Military Intelligence.

But it was *Walter* Ernest Butler, not Bill. I'd actually been writing to him long before I stumbled on your address in an old copy of the New Dimensions magazine. It has been a lifelong regret that I never met him, although as I wrote in an essay about Parallel Lives somewhere something akin to 'I' might have linked up in other ways.

And I note you seem to fear, in the reincarnation sense, getting 'shunted back here for a long long time'. Bill, Bill, Bill… in a few years time you will meet Marcia Pickands and tell her *exactly* where you will be reborn, and soon, somewhere in America. Will you get this notion from me, here, now, in 2023 as I lurk behind your head in 1983? Odd thought that. I will later learn the details that you passed on privately to Marcia, from Marcia herself, but I've long since deliberately forgotten them – no small feat that! I wouldn't want any small child being 'recognised' as Bill Gray reborn. There are still those who feel that the Tibetans got the wrong boy when it came to finding the newly-incarnated Dalai Lama. And if Robert Cochrane *did return* via your friend, I hope he has peace and kindness and no madness in his life *this* time.

Best

Alan

Wm. G. Gray

14. Bennington St.
Cheltenham
Glos. GL50 4ED

Telephone

(0242) 24129

30 August 1983

Dear Alan,
Thanks for your letter but I'm afraid I can't help very much. I was never very close to Dion Fortune, being a teenager when I came across her in London, and she seemed very formidable to me. My own 'Master' was a Rosicrucian who had been a close associate of Papus. It wasn't until just after the War that I joined the Inner Light officially and wasn't with them long and by that time Dion Fortune was dead. By then the Inner Light was at a real 'low', and I've had nothing to do with it ever since. They had got hooked on Scientology, and were being run by a real shit called Chichester, some relative of the yachtsman I understand.

    I can tell you incident concerning Crowley. Apparently DF had written him in reference to a proposed invokation of a demon or supernatural called Tapthartherath (or near enough) who was supposed to be an Hermetic sort of spirit. Crowley instructed his secretary (Gerald Yorke) to find out if there was anything DF particularly disliked, It appeared that she disliked fish. So Crowley sent her solemn instructions that in order to invoke T-whatshisname properly, the only way was to eat masses and masses of fish first, Apparently DF fell for this stupid. ploy and ate enough fish to make herself sick, but old T-thing never showed even the tip of a nose. Crowley's only remark apparently was 'Bloody stupid woman'. Crowley was like that, and after his early experience with his mother I can't say I blame him. Mrs Crowley was more to blame than her pathetic son,

    So far as I know, Dion Fortune and Crowley didn't actually meet, You'll find that most occultists hate each others guts for fear the other guy will hog the publicity they crave, or the adulation they can't do without.

'Dr Taverner' so far as I know, was based on her own husband whom you'll remember was a. psychiatrist, but only loosely based, He was a very handsome man in the photo I have,

DF did have that strange dichotomy between her 'Pagan' self and 'Christian' self, which I always felt was at the root of her eventual leukaemia., She could never reconcile the two sides of herself. And her views on sex would now be considered very comical by even an average person.

The one thing DF <u>did</u> of outstanding service, was to emphasise the importance of the Western Inner Tradition, which I have faithfully tried to uphold against claims of all gurus, mahatmas, yogis, and other oriental invaders of our Inner Space. Until she spoke out, nobody was doing very much or would even admit that we <u>had</u> a Tradition second to none. For Gods sake give the woman every credit for <u>that</u>. She may have been a million things that weren't <u>quite</u>, but for her service to Western esotericism she deserves a hell of a lot of credit, Let us say she dragged it into the twentieth century and updated its outworn phraseology. Pity she didn't live longer, although the chances are that if she had, she'd have ballsed up the good she did.

My own Sangreal series are coming along quite well, Nos. 1 and 2 out this year, 3 about December, 4 by next Summer, and I've just today finished No 5, the Sangreal Tarot system, Nothing else is trying to break through, but who knows what might next year after I've been to South Africa again,

Anyway the 'occult situation' has totally changed since Dion Fortune's time and what was valid then would not apply now at all, I hope you have some success with your work. By the way, are you registering for PLR's? I've done so, and am British Author No 007361 on the list, (love the 907 bit) It probably won't be worth more than about £1 per year to me if that, but it could be worth more to you.

Sorry I can't help more with anecdotes about DF, but I didn't really know her either well or in the least closely, Just shove in all you can get and invent the rest like most professional writers usually do. DF would have hated it.

Anyway, nice to have heard from you and all the best of luck.

Bill

Trowbridge Library   28th February 2023

Hello Bill,
A sign of the times, this. Am looking at that last letter of yours in the atrium of Trowbridge's excellent library, to which I was connected when I ran a specialist Mobile Library based across the road. It's bitterly cold outside and the tabloids are predicting a Beast from the East to sweep across and bring snow. There's already 14 inches fallen in Mallorca, in the supposedly balmy Mediterranean, which will no doubt be hailed as yet another sign of global warming. But it's cozy enough here and will save on our heating bills at home. Plus I've just learned that the human heart comprises two atriums: the right atrium receives deoxygenated blood from the veins of the body, while the left atrium oxygenated blood from the pulmonary vein. As ever, if I look for it, there's always magickal symbolism to be found.

And I will use the 'k'. On perhaps my last visit you asked me apropos of nothing if I knew why Crowley spelled it that way? *Yes*, I said, as I'd recently read Crowley's own words on the matter, *It was because...* However you frowned and wouldn't let me continue, but gave me a long, recently intuited, but substantially accurate explanation.

In the far corner of this large atrium and also in the memories of my heart, there's a mass of toddlers singing about the *Wheels on the Bus* going 'round and 'round, and this is heavenly, better than any of the Perpetual Choirs that they used to have in medieval times.

Can you remember, Bill, in the good old days when you *had* to whisper in libraries, and what Dion Fortune might have described as 'widows and grey-bearded ancients' would put their fingers to their lips like Harpocrates and go *Sssssh*! I recall that Eliphas Levi, whom you believe reincarnated as your teacher 'ENH', enjoined magicians to Know, Will, Dare – and above all Keep Silent. Now, it seems, all the wannabe magicians aspire to Know, Will, Dare – and above all get Ticks on every variety of Social Media that evolves. It seems that you're not so much judged these days by initiation marks in your aura, but by the number of Likes on Facebook, or Twitter, or Instagram or blogs and vlogs, or whatever else is coming into existence now.

And it's just struck me that if I burbled to you yesterday about a subtle phoneyness of many (if not all) magicians, then perhaps it's more to do with the magical technique of 'acting As If', which is not very far removed from the initiatory secret of places like Silicone Valley, where you're enjoined to 'Fake it until you Make it.'

How things change have changed eh?

And it's odd, too (some sort of synchronicity?), but as the wind whistles through the automatic doors at the entrance to the library, arriving from the East like Mary Poppins, I've just received on my phone an email from 'David Conway', perhaps the last of the Celebrity Magicians. I know he will bristle at that term, which is why I use it. Conway and I seem to have developed a mutually cheeky and admiring relationship over the years, and while he might be far more intellectual and knowledgeable than *moi*, I'm definitely more handsome. I personally think he should adopt me as his Magical Son and bequeath me a huge fortune. At the moment he is working on the second part of his autobiography, featuring his own teacher in Magic, the Welsh healer and subtle magus figure Mathonwy, so in differing ways we're working in parallel.

You yourself knew and worked with those who became Celebrity Magicians of the even Older School: Emile Napoleon Hauenstein who once worked with the legendary Papus, and whose material was filched by Harvey Spencer Lewis of AMORC; the so-called Founding Mothers of modern Wicca Pat Crowther and Doreen Valiente; The Chief Druid Thomas Maughan; Gareth Knight, Robert Cochrane and many others unknown to the outer worlds. And R.J. Stewart of course, who is still going strong, and who you and Bobbie always thought was an ancient soul - although you fell out with him as you did everyone, in this case I think over the tinny sound of the keyboard he used in the recording of your Rollright Ritual. You felt he should have organised the massive organ in Bath Abbey, near where he lived.

You might have enjoyed Conway's writings. There is a wickedness of observation and waspish sting in his *bons mots* (though not quite as classy as my own *mots justes*) that would make you chuckle. You were never homophobic Bill, and spoke fondly of an all-gay coven you knew about. And while you have been branded racist, as a man of your place and times, I heard that toward the end of your life you had the sort of deep *deep* revelation that goes beyond mere personality and conditioning and Mind, exploding within you the personal Gnosis that we are *All* One. After that, no-one *can* be racist. Besides, all humans came from Africa in the first place, which is maybe why, to my knowledge, your only working Sangreal Sodality is still going there.

To me, that was so fucking obvious. All. Is. One. I could have told you that years ago, but you wouldn't have listened. Maybe you're listening now? At the back of your brain?

I don't mean to sound superior. As you've just said about DF, you faithfully tried to uphold the importance of the Western Inner Tradition, against claims of all gurus, mahatmas, yogis, and other invaders of our Inner Space. As a once long-haired hippyish child of *my* times, I remember the 60's and 70's when everything spiritual was Eastern, and everything Eastern was spiritual. And present readers should know that my first wife, with whom I am still in amicable contact, was Chinese. No-one can flog me about hidden racism because of my connection with you. Though I could certainly flog myself about my own young ignorance.

Oh and you mention the dreaded Arthur Chichester. At your initiation into the Inner Light you had a vision of him as leading an *auto-da-fé* during the Inquisition. And in one of your very first letters to me when I was a teen, you described him as – I'll never forget the phrase or its rhythms - '...a Jesuit-trained ex-intelligence officer with a severely warped personality'. To Dion, he was her Sun Priest and successor. Yet your own personal nemesis Basil Wilby, aka 'Gareth Knight', who worked with Chichester a lot, came to wonder if he was not in fact a Jesuit plant (or do I mean *agent provocateur*?). He ceremonially burned Dion's Magical Diaries and anything personal after her death in 1946, determinedly broke up the truly magical curriculums and grades, and turned the Lodge into a group that was merely Devotional. Certainly the channelled teachings at that time were *pitiful*. Chichester was not racist but definitely homophobic; gays were not allowed to take entry into the Lodge unless they got straight! He perhaps turned a blind eye or didn't know that Mrs Evans was said to have indulged herself with some girl-on-girl action after Penry left and Maiya Tranchell Hayes appeared. Or else he was too busy having fun doing some 'Polarity Magic' with other women at the nudist camp near Bricketts Wood, where the IL maintained a chalet named 'Avalon'. 'Polarity Magic' is what posh people call Sex Magic, though perhaps they should add the 'k' as Crowley would have done.

Have I said too much?

I believe that Basil Wilby, who died fairly recently, in his later years returned the Lodge to its original level and it is now, once more, working *real* Magic with effective initiatory structures; so that by the time you achieve the Third Degree (if indeed you ever do) you will be able to make direct personal contact with the Inner Plane Adeptii, as they once called them, and thence go your own inner way.

You probably still wouldn't like them though.

Yes, but Dion Fortune and Crowley did meet. You can see details in my comparative biography *Aleister Crowley and Dion Fortune – Logos of the Aeon, Shakti of the Age*. And Dion's *Dr Taverner* stories were based upon her own teacher, Theodore William Carte Moriarty, an Irishman who, oddly enough, also had a South African background and was a senior Freemason, as far as I can remember. I haven't got the energy to climb up into my loft and unearth the books and documents. These days, from the quietude of your own home, or in your local library, or even on your smart phone, you can google what you need instantly.

Yes, Dr. Thomas Penry Evans, a working class lad from Llanelli, was a good looking fella. Christine Hartley, who was *my* true teacher, insisted that Merl, as they called him, was *the* Magus in the lodge, a truly Great Soul.

On the best day we ever had, neither Crowley nor Dion, nor Chichester nor me nor thee, were ever in the same league as Penry Evans.

All the best

alan

Wm. G. Gray
14. Bennington St.
Cheltenham
Glos. GL50 4ED

Telephone

(0242) 24129

16th September 1983

Dear Alan,

Thanks for your letter and cheque which I'm returning with a copy of the only photo I have of DF and her husband. Taken at Chalice Orchard Glastonbury, which I believe is now owned by Geoffrey Ashe. Have it with my blessing, I've got copies.

    In my time the mysterious 'Inner Head' of the IL was supposed to be St Thomas More, who was always referred to in whispers as 'The C'. meaning of course the Chancellor. Something I was always suspicious of because he always gave such stuffy, tendentious and 'moral' messages reminiscent of some priggish nonconformist preacher 'exhorting' sinners. Entirely and absolutely humourless, whereas in life More was a witty and most cheerful chap. I have no information about Lord Eldon at all, or about ancient Spartan kings or ancient Egyptian High Priests, which most occult Orders were claiming if it wasn't Atlanteans. I imagine nowadays its all beings from Outer Space. I strongly distrust all 'Spirit ' on principle. Especially my own, whose names I don't even know, and wouldn't believe if they told me. They are very far from being sweetness and light in the Spiritualist sense of the word.

    Nor do I know a damn thing about Col. Seymour. As a matter of fact I knew little or nowt about the personalities behind the IL, beyond the fact they were more or less kept going by a Canadian magnate called Bill Elmore, and as I told you I got out when they went all peculiar with Scientology. I don't have good memories of the IL at all. Or I should say the <u>people</u> who composed it. You probably know more about them than I do, or have heard more.

    Their Spartan contact would just about account for their stuffiness, lack of feeling, general offhandedness and incivility. In fact about the only good word I can say for the Inner Light is that they were financially honest, and their leaders certainly weren't in it for the money like American occultists are. Their Inner contacts were genuine, but not very warm or welcoming.

I'm told the IL are still going 'but only just' whatever that might mean. I'm totally out of the 'occult scene' from any social angles nowadays, and try to keep clear apart from my South African and Brazilian contacts.

Your Xerox of Lord Eldon does keep remind me of Walter Scott. What was the Eldon's family name, do you know?

I do remember the old Chief Druid telling me that years ago when he was making contact with all the various heads of Occult Orders in Britain with the suggestion that there should be some kind of working liaison among them all, the only single one of them in the least bit interested was Dion Fortune, but of course nothing came of it.

I've remembered an apocryphal about her which might amuse you. During the 1st World War when she was a Land Girl, she was having a row with the formers she was working for about the money they owed her and didn't pay. She just happened to have the huge bunch of keys for all the various doors on that farm, Eventually she got the cover off the shit-pit and stood. on the edge with the keys poised over the poop. She then threatened that if they didn't cough up forthwith, she would hurl the keys into the crap and they would have to fish them out after she'd left. They paid! And she left triumphantly.

I've got the typescript of my Tarot book away to Weisers about a week ago, but it'll take a couple of years to come out I should think. Rather to my surprise I hear Weisers have rejected two books by Sarah Carter in the USA. She's a delightful and knowledgeable person, so I can't quite imagine why and don't like to ask Don Weiser though I know him personally. It's probably a question of money, because Weisers aren't a big concern at all. In fact there's only two of them really, Don and his wife, Betty Lundsted. He does have an extremely good reputation for financial honesty and only publishing 'solid' occult material. None of the commercial quick-selling trash like 'Raise Demons for pleasure and profit', 'Masturbation by Magic', and the like crap. Unluckily he's about the only publisher in the USA (and they have far fewer occult publishers than we have) who is reliable...

I'm jut beginning to get enquiries in this country about the Sangreal Sodality, which I've got to deal with. Nothing worth while. The whole idea is to work the <u>opposite</u> way to usual organisations, the same as the original Rosicrucians did. N0 'central organisation' in this world at all. Everybody forms up their own autonomous group under the aegis of the Sangreal and eventually they can all communicate with each if they want to or stay as a purely private concern.

There can be an entire Group of just one person. Providing they don't <u>exceed</u> twelve people, why not. It'll take maybe another hundred years or more. Maybe I'll just be in time to catch it in my next birth.

We desperately need to avert such idiotic and ridiculous rumours that the Sangreal Concept is in any way aligned with with or sympathetic to Neo-Nazism, the KKK, or any such human (or should I say anti-human) outlooks. The Sangreal firstly aligns us with <u>ourselves</u> and thereby whatever human grouping we belong with by birth and breeding. Then it aligns all those Groups with our entire species, and after that with others in their order throughout the entire Cosmos. Everything arranged in correct and proper order. What is wrong with that????

                All good wishes,

                    fraternally,

Bill

Leykers Cafe   March 4th 2023
Wiltshire.

Hello Bill,
I'm scribbling this in a caff and will transfer it onto the pc when I get home. As I've often explained at length and even *ad nauseum*, I don't do anything remotely like Meditation; I *do* sit in cafés with one half of my mind reading the news, and the other half not quite on this planet – at least according to my wife. It works for me. If there'd been no-one else around I might cry out: *I am perplexed!* Weren't they supposed to be Crowley's last words? Or am I thinking of Oscar Wilde? I instantly remember some bright spark – I think it might have been the brilliantly bitchy literary critic Cyril Connolly – defining Crowley as the man who bridged the gap between Oscar Wilde and Hitler.

I am perplexed! because I had an odd night, unable to sleep because of a stinking, fluey sort of cold. So I went to the spare room and browsed the internet on my phone and also scanned through what I've written in my note pad so far, for any obvious bloopers or inelegant prose. I don't want David Conway tut-tutting if he ever gets to read the finished product. I emailed him the previous page, to see if he'd take umbrage. Unfortunately he didn't. He's already sent an instant reply, which I'm reading now on my phone, trying not to drop it into the beans on toast.

> *Alan...*
> *As Phineas Barnum said, there's no such thing as bad publicity.*
> *No objections, - well, apart from the fact that you'd never heard of mot juste until I mentioned it (and even now seem unsure of its meaning).*
> *I speak of public libraries in the new book, mentioning the frail, softly spoken Miss Sims "a disciple of Mrs Baker Eddy" who'd allow the twelve year old me to borrow occulty books, subject to her approval, from the grown-ups' section. (My contemporaries gorged on Biggles and Blyton.)*

> *Just turned down a request from Ken Russell's film-maker son to participate in a documentary about the swinging 'seventies. They edit these things and one risks seeming dafter than one is. Besides, I seldom swung. My Welsh conscience wouldn't let me.*
> *Get some fresh air. Municipal reading rooms are for the unwashed and the indigent*
> *On second thoughts...*
> *B.*

But Bill, *I am perplexed!* because I wrote in my last letter to you that Basil Wilby had died 'fairly recently'. I would have sworn that I heard of his death only a couple of weeks ago. In fact, as one of his pupils just noted on some Facebook pop-up, he died almost exactly a year ago, on March 1st. Of course it's the age thing: these days, time flies. I suppose, in the context of yourself, this really is the end of some sort of Gravian Aeon. Your spleen was legendary, but in the case of Basil Wilby not at all mutual. He still published your books, even when you fell out. And now his daughter Rebsie has published even more of them via Skylight Press. Yet there is no-one left who once evoked the hey-day of all this.

I did love that sentence on the 16 September: 'I strongly distrust all 'Spirits' on principle. Especially my own, whose names I don't even know, and wouldn't believe if they told me.' That's not what you would expect! On the other hand Basil himself told me that that was not *quite* true, and that you knew – or were able to apply names to – your own 'Guides' full well.

I say 'apply names' because, although I'm a rotten psychic, there's no doubt that energies/ entities have often swamped me, but working on all sorts of levels in differing ways, to the extent that I've sometimes felt used. That's why I always loved Walt Whitman's poem *I Sing the Body Electric!* because that felt like me at times. It was never easy, and my still abundant hair often seemed to stand on end with what coursed through. But did they 'guide' me? Did they buggery. Did they give me wise counsel? Bollocks to that an' all. Which is why I much prefer the term 'Inner Contacts'. Perhaps I'm being unfair. Perhaps its not the intellectual content of any communication that is important, so much as the actual *presence* – the knowledge that you're not alone in the multiverse. Certainly this worked out for me via endless serendipities and bizarre happenstance, as I've written about elsewhere.

I always said to Basil that I would be quite happy for him to 'come through' to me, but I've had not the slightest whisper. However, Bill, I would not want *you* to come through in any way, even though we agreed upon a key-word that would confirm your identity if any psychic medium picked up you, or a simulacrum, and tried to get me to champion your Sangreal stuff. Now I'm your age, I'm no longer in awe of you - as you can probably tell.

I note that the Inner Light, under Chichester, only turned to Thomas More after the film *A Man for All Seasons* came out, wherein Paul Schofield showed More as a man of enormous rectitude and principle and got an Oscar for it. But Bill... Thomas More was a shit. He tortured, and/or encouraged torture, of heretics. And what was their heresy, pray tell? Translating the *New Testament* into English, so that the common man could hear the Word without relying on the bent and corrupt priests filtering it all through the Latin and Greek.

If I've ever been overshadowed by the egregore of the Fraternity of the Inner Light (as I think I have, though never having been a member) then I cleave to Seymour and Hartley's notion that the Chancellor was Lord Eldon, whose energies also seem to have nudged me many times.

I did send you the typescript of what became *Dancers to the Gods*, containing the Magical Diaries of Christine Hartley and Kim Seymour from their time within the FIL, and you were impressed. *Their* Chancellor, 'Lord Eldon', was indeed John Scott, a fellow Northumbrian from the Holy City of Newcastle on Tyne. Is there something going on at levels of DNA here Bill? I don't totally cleave to the bog-standard ideas of reincarnation these days. I suspect that ancient impulses/memories/nudgings can also come via tribal DNA, if there is such a thing. Often tied to Spirit of Place. I could take you to places in Dorset where it would be hard not to have a shivering *frisson* about Lord Eldon, or 'Old Bags' as Seymour and Hartley called him. And yes, Eldon's family fancied they had links with Walter Scott and even with the medieval wizard Michael Scot, to whom Dante gave an admiring mention.

And finally, I must take a deep breath, pause, and then confess... I've never had the slightest interest in your Sangreal Sodality as defined by you or anyone else. Sorry 'bout that. You say: 'It'll take maybe another hundred years or more' before it all takes off.

Bill, Bill, Bill… it **won't**. To me, your series of Sangreal books with their ponderous rituals were a hundred years after their time. They were old-fashioned when they were written. In fact I've always thought the Holy Grail itself was a spiritual trap, but I wrote about that in my collection of essays called *Short Circuits*.

Which reminds me that when I did *Searching for Sulis* I did have an encounter with a rather tawdry end-of-the-pier spirit/energy presenting as the Fisher King.

I'd forgotten all about that!

That's another age thing.

Best

Alan

Wm. G. Gray
14. Bennington St.
Cheltenham
Glos. GL50 4ED

Telephone

(0242) 24129

7th December 1983

Dear Alan

Thanks for yours, pics (how like Crowley) and news. For Christ's sake don't send anything just yet.

   1. Bobbie is ill and the Dr. hasn't determined what it is yet.
   2. I've had to cancel my South African trip on that account.
   3. My roof is being replaced and the roof is full of mess and will take a month to straighten afterwards.
   4. I'm not well myself.
   5. This typewriter is breaking down.
   6. Weisers have all sorts of problems for me, and
   7. I'm not sure what else is happening.

In short, we are in SHIT for the unforeseeable future.

Just had the galleys of reprinted TREE OF EVIL. So that'll be out again.

With the whole of Xmas buggered to hell, I'd rather not bother with your spare MS and couldn't do it justice anyway.

You seem to have uncovered a nice can of worms. Yes, I had seen the pic of DF as a kid.

All the best for now, but I assure you I'm in no state to write an objective letter. Give me another month and then send to find out if I'm still in the land of the living.

At least if Carr Collins didn't like my Tarot book, Weisers <u>did</u>, but are hanging on to see what to title it.

Sorry about all this. It would all happen in one lump.

                    Fraternally

                    Bill

Melksham Library   6th March 2023

Hello again Bill,

I'm not sure how I replied to that last letter. I probably made noises of sympathy and support without feeling any of them. I was having difficult times then myself, although in truth that's no excuse.

When I had my heart attack I was flown through the skies by helicopter ambulance; I had no glimpse of the Tunnel of Light and angel guides that so many have experienced. But in the Intensive Care Ward I did spend the hours looking back on my life. Many seers have insisted that after death the soul is able to look back upon every aspect of its life without judgement, with complete detachment, and then makes a decision as to where and when it will reincarnate in order to balance out its lessons.

I'm inclined to believe that. Before I entered into my own mother's womb, I – or some sort of conscious glob approximating to the notion of 'I', looked down upon my parents and decided they were the ones I needed for this next life, beginning in November 1951…

I think that the heart attack has made me re-assess myself now before I go into the Chamber of Maat and realise that, on the whole, I've been an arrogant, self-important, un-loyal shit. A memory of something the Duke of Wellington said at the end of his glory-filled life has just floated in, so I must go with it… The General who was unbeaten on the battlefields, and the Iron Duke who also became Prime Minister, was asked if there was anything he regretted. After brief consideration he confessed: 'I wish I'd given more praise.'

For me, I wish I'd been kinder. *And* given more praise.

So Bill, I can tell you now that Bobbie, of whom I was very fond and was *never* afraid, will outlive you, though only briefly, and that you will both be ready and right glad to go when your times come…

                     thoughtful, musing hugs

                     Alan

Wm. G. Gray
14. Bennington St.
Cheltenham
Glos. GL50 4ED

Telephone

(0242) 24129

16th February 1984½

Dear Alan,

Thanks for the pic of DF's school outing, but which one is she????

    I've just got back from South Africa today and am trying to clear my backlog of mail. Amongst other letters I found one from Carr Collins, (the Texan millionaire who sometimes backs my books.) and believe it or not he wants information about Dion Fortune for a book he is thinking of doing on her. (Which I didn't give him.) People all over the place are suddenly getting interested in DF and her work. So there is obviously a market waiting which you'd better hurry like hell to produce and get those concerned to put their backs into it.

    This obviously means something. Whether she is reincarnated or what I'm not sure, but the certainty is that people are getting interested in the Western Inner Tradition and wanting to know more about it and who promulgated it as protagonists. They'll probably try the same with me about fifty years after I'm dead, and there won't be an interesting thing to say.

    Even my South African friend has written a book which has me in a lot. I slightly doubt if he will get it taken by Weisers, but one never knows. I was helping him with the English which only wanted an odd word here and there altered.

    Weisers have reissued several of my old books at last, but the two coming out will take more time. At least I've got a theme for another book, but I suspect it mightn't get taken. Anyhow I'll enjoy writing it, and I never wrote for the sake of the money anyway.

    So, all I really wrote this note to say was GET ON WITH IT, - AND FAST.

                        Bless you.

Bill

The Garden Office   7ᵗʰ March 7ᵗʰ 2023

Hello Bill,
Well, you've certainly perked up! I note, for the very first time, the almost whimsical touch of giving the date as 1984½. And that you end with 'Bless You'.

Yes, there was a race to write the first biography of 'Dion Fortune', that I outlined in *Me, MySelf and Dion Fortune*. As I was looking through it only yesterday I was bewildered to see that I had dedicated it to: 'Jackie, Alexander and Pat'. *Jackie, Alexander and Pat? Jackie, Alexander and Pat?* Who the fuck are they!? I kept asking myself. It only came to me in the wee small hours, as so much of my stuff does, that these were (and possibly still are), the three people who shared the Wardenship of the 'Society of the Inner Light', as it is today.

I liked them Bill. They invited me for tea! In a sense it was like coming home, although I'd never been before or met them before, though deep deep inside me it will always be the '*Fraternity* of the Inner Light', called thus from the ancient of days. There seems to have been a part of me that was present when that photo of her and Penry was taken. I am certain that this was not at Chalice Orchard as the legend goes, but in a London park, just after their civil wedding.

Am I too old to join them now? I'd work through the initial teachings and not play the big 'I Am', as John Scott and other Northumbrians would say, but I wouldn't bash myself with their seminal text 'The Cosmic Doctrine', that I don't think anyone *really* understands. Or if they do, they must be a bit weird. I doubt if even the inner plane communicators themselves really understood what they were downloading into Dr. Moriarty. I don't think anyone's spiritual progress will be impeded by putting it aside. If you want to train the mind, then Stephen Hawkins 'A Brief History of Time' will do the same thing.

But I don't understand that one either.

So Bill, I can tell you that YES, you will soon meet a woman whom you will be quite certain is Dion Fortune reborn. Personally, by that time, I will have made contact with several other women who are also quite certain that *they* are DF reborn.

Bye for now, Bill, I've got another streamingly snotty cold and must go crash…

But... I must add something extra here…

I dipped into the next couple of letters from you, the first for the **29th January 1984** and see that Bobbie has been sorted out by the local hospital. Her problems were caused by 'Hyperacidosis', and you write: 'So she'll have to pack in smoking, keep upright and watch everything she eats. Cause? A lifetime of sitting in a bad position (crouched), smoking somewhat heavily, and ill-temper which makes the acid. Not too difficult to do something about anyway.'

Easier said than done, Bill...

And then you add, equally brightly: 'All building work finished now, so I'll start to do a few house jobs, but at 70+ with arthritis I'm not so fast or so capable as I was a few years ago.'

Believe you me, I know that story now too! There's all sorts of stuff we need to do in our old house in Wiltshire with its long and narrow garden, and I have to carefully manage my own energies after The Event, as I think of my heart attack. Unlike you I'm famously useless at any kind of DIY.

And then there was one on the **15th February 1984** wherein you say very flattering things about a MS I'd sent you, but I can't remember which one. Perhaps *Gate of Moon*? And you add:

'Anyway it was very nice to see you again and notice how much you have developed since last time [1974]. Lets say you've improved with age and experience however bitter that may have been at the time. I'm also happy to hear that you've met up with what sounds like a suitable mate. Things seem to be going as reasonably as anyone can expect life to run in this worrisome world.'

The suitable mate was my second wife, Michelle, and the next letter from you was your very long and loving response to the dreadful times I was having when my Mam was diagnosed with final state cancer, and then we lost our first baby in nightmare circumstances on what should have been our wedding day on March 10th 1984.

Your letter is the longest you ever sent, but I include it here in full to show the world that under the tough and often scary Gravian carapace was a big hearted, warm-hearted fella who was both kind to me and gave praise…

Alan

Wm. G. Gray

**14. Bennington St.
Cheltenham
Glos. GL50 4ED**

Telephone

(0242) 24129

3rd May 1984

Dear Alan,

I''m desolated to hear your news. You are quite naturally asking the same question we all do in similar plight, - WHY? If only a rhyme or reason could be found for it, things would be easier to bear, but it is the apparent senselessness and purposelessness of it all that hurts so much. Of course there isn't really one reason for it it, but a hell of a lot of little reasons which have coincided through a Time factor, and its this co-incidence which you are feeling in connection with yourself, so what you are really asking is why NOW?

Lets isolate all the incidents singly. Obviously your mother (God be with her) was developing a tumour anyway which would have come by itself as could have happened to anyone, so there can he no connection between that and yourself whatever, although you will naturally feel emotionally involved. I don't know the circumstances of your wife's miscarriage, (God be with her too) but I shouldn't suppose you were in any way responsible apart from being the father of her child in the first place. If your job is in any way connected with the civil service or Local Government, the whole of that structure is being thoroughly bitched and buggered about by reorganisations, and everybody is being affected by this. So it isn't anything you've done, and cruel Fate is NOT hitting at you by inflicting casualties on other humans connected with you. It doesn't work that way. What it has done is give you the type of mind which is capable of seeing beyond the tip of its nose and wonder if there is a connection between all these things happening to all those people. Which of course there is, and that connection is Life itself..While we are in this world horrible things happen to us, but the vast majority are caused by other human beings or the workings of natural forces which we have not yet come to terms with.

The 'Gods' cannot interfere with the workings of those forces because they ARE the forces themselves, If they are part of Conscious

Creation they have to follow the Patterns they have created. All humans can do is hope to change the course of some of these Energies by providing alternative Paths through themselves. Whether you call this science or Magic it amounts to the same thing on different levels.

You are wondering if you've stirred anything up by writing 'magical' books. No more nor less than other writers of the same genre, (including myself) and look at all their lives. Dion Fortune dead before she reached 50 from leukaemia, a blood dyscrasia she probably inherited. Crowley mostly from a life of poor living due to drugs. Mathers from drink and stupid disregard of health. It would be interesting to study personal lives of all these literati and see what happened to them. For my own part, I never seriously believed. in what I came to call 'The Opposition' until I tried to get the RITE OF LIGHT or Sangreal Sacrament published. Then so many odd happenings occurred to prevent this for such a long period that I became convinced there must be something trying its best to abort the work. Nevertheless, once the thing was out in print and on tape, that was the end of the opposition.

I was thinking of Mike and Marion Parker whose baby burned to death a few years back. They'd written a book on Western Temples (not a bad one as well). Mike tried to tell himself afterwards that the baby hadn't meant to live very long anyway. I've no idea what happened to them after that, My own mother had a massive stroke at 64, never came out of hospitals after that and died at 73 of the usual pneumonia with complications. That however was entirely due to natural causes and of her own making, Endless people including me warned her again and again, yet she took not the slightest notice and went on with her totally wrong diet, oversmoking, and massive weight. And paid a bitter price for it in the end. Arnold Crowther died of lung cancer due to heavy smoking and always keeping a cigarette in the corner of his mouth virtually all day. My father on the other hand. who did smoke a pipe but not excessively and kept to a very plain but mostly boiled, (never fried) food, lived. in perfect health up to 86 and dropped dead of coronary occlusion one morning while getting his breakfast. Lucky chap.

So get it out of your head that the 'Gods' are picking on you personally. They aren't. And what sort of 'Opposition' do you suppose would oppose any book you have yet written or are likely to write? No, it is simply that quite a number of unhappy events seem to have coincided in your recent experience of life, and it is the coincidence itself bothering you. I have found this sort of happening comes to so many people everywhere until it piles up to an absolute crescendo, then all of a sudden seems to stop, and very little happens to them again for years, It seems to be simply a Life-pattern which affects intelligent and sensitive people far more than others as you might expect.

Several people (including myself) have found it helps if you honestly feel the 'Gods' are treating you like apiece of shit to stand up for yourself and have a go back. In fact I've written a special Rite for it calling it the 'Rite of Reproach'. It is only for use on very rare occasions, and I've only done it about twice in my life - but it worked. In the old days people would go in their Temples and really tear loose at their 'Gods', telling them just what they thought of such ill-treatment. That'll be published some time this summer, but I could send you a tape of the thing if you'd like. I don't have an actual script, Its only for when you get to the absolute end of your tether.

Mike Jamieson was having a very similar run to yourself a while back, and eventually came to visit me when we ran through the Sangreal Sacrament together. Some few weeks later the golden opportunity he'd been hoping for came through, and now he's gone to live in the Isle of Man where I hope he will prosper. (He's an air pilot by profession)

Personally I've never had a lot of trust in my 'guides or Inners'. As long as they can get the work out of you, OK, but when you've served their purpose - that's it. On the other hand the work has to _be_ done, so you get on with it because it's on your plate so to speak. Anyway I did the best I could, and you are certainly going ahead with your share.

Bobbie says to send you her most sincere sympathy, and her advice is to live the way you want and bugger the Gods. I wouldn't endorse this altogether myself, but I know what she means. In other words let the worm turn a bit. That's what I wrote that Rite for. I'd had about a gutful.

Life can be absolutely bloody can't it? The one consolation is that we can't live here forever. The important thing is to try and fulfil some useful purpose while we can, and that is something you seem to be doing. What about your poor wife? She must be feeling terrible. Do try to convey our sincerest condolences. Words are pretty useless for offering sympathy, but all our kind thoughts are with you both, and I will personally pray for you that some kind of good will come out or all this trouble in the end. There just has to be something of value in the experience, dreadful as that may sound, and I do most sincerely hope you will gain whatever it might be. Perhaps inspiration for some particularly valuable book in maybe a few years time which you couldn't have written otherwise? You will certainly find out eventually even if that's a long way off yet. Do let me know what develops.

Bill

The Garden Office   10th March 2023

Dear Bill – although I think 'Dear' is not the best epithet to use after your last letter, though 'Dearest' might be a bit too much mawkish. When I opened and read that missive for the first time since I received then folded it away, 40 years ago, I was startled. Although 'startled' is also not the best epithet. I seem to have wiped your words from my mind. With a memory that never forgets slights, no matter how trivial, nor yet any kind of praise, no matter how undeserved, this was all new. The events you refer to were so catastrophic that I must have sealed them away within my own personal *mastaba* – a word that means 'eternal home' – leaving them to lie there in the forever darkness like a pharaoh's mummy, stiff and unmoving and eternally dead.

You were kind Bill. You gave praise.

And I was also startled because, as I write this to comment, it is also March 10th. I suppose the date-match suggests to me that everything, including past and future, is all happening NOW.

Did I ever get redress back then in the simultaneous 1984? Well, exactly one year later to the very hour, daughter Zoe was born. I'm not sure if that balances anything though, or if the fucking 'Guides' were trying to say sorry in their *time-means-nothing-to-us* sort of way.

You said about the 'Guides' (always in inverted commas) 'As long as they can get the work out of you, OK, but when you've served their purpose - that''s it. On the other hand the work has to be done, so you get on with it because it's on your plate so to speak.' How true. You're not the only magician I've met since to note that 'They' have their own agenda.

Enough already. That day and the aftermath is still painful. I'm never sure that 'closure' is ever as possible as modern therapies promise.

You mention the Rite of Reproach. I didn't recall that either. I rarely do 'rites' of any kind. That's partly due to the inspiration of Murry Hope, whom you and Bobbie knew as 'Jacqueline Thorburn', the founder of the small but once-influential group 'The Atlanteans', based in Cheltenham. I suppose you might call mine the Rite of Rebalance, or even the Rite of Redress – if only for the alliteration. I've used this often. The actual written words aren't important, so much as the inward intent (I learned that from Murry Hope too).

Basically I have what I now call a Good Think and then approach Thoth, the Lord of Justice, with a simple plea. It goes something like:

> If it is right and proper and part of Maat that this should be happening to me, then I accept. Help me learn the lessons I need from this, and help me get through it.
>
> But if it is **NOT** right and proper, and things in my life *have* become unbalanced and unfair, then please redress the issues.

This should not be done casually. There needs to be intensity of feeling behind the invocation, as well as a visualisation of Thoth, if indeed that 'God' is your exemplar of Justice.

Did this work for me, you ask?

Yes, once spectacularly so in a way that I will never tell. BUT... I noticed that one several occasions when I used this the distressing events actually intensified! Presumably this was because it *was* 'right and proper' for me to be flogged, as I thought of it. Then it all stopped, as unseen dues were somehow paid, and the Scales balanced.

Looking back though, from this age of 71½, I do feel that in the oddest of ways my life *has* been guided. Who or What was 'guiding' or protecting me? Well, sometimes during all the recent post-heart-attack and pre-death speculations I wonder if it was actually Me!

If, during The Review when I relive every single micro-second of the life I've just finished, perhaps I nudged mySelf into making choices, avoiding relationships and jobs and choices that glistered but would have been disastrous. Perhaps – but only perhaps - mySelf helped Little Me avoid the many pitfalls I could have known.

Though I suppose, Bill, this mad notion only works because I'm a happy 71½ year old, with the sort of life I've always wanted...

Anyway, I'm still somewhat frazzled from the shock of seeing that letter, but thank you for it wholeheartedly. It's pissing down now and getting dark, and I will go indoors and watch something mindless on the telly. (What you once called the Idiot Box in the Corner, and swore *never* to have. Although I do know that one evening when I visited, you were talking about the historical errors in Charlton Heston's *The War*

Lord that had been on the telly the previous night. So I reckon Bobbie – God bless her - got her way over that one…)

Best

Alan

Wm. G. Gray
14. Bennington St.
Cheltenham
Glos. GL50 4ED

Telephone

(0242) 24129

9 AUG 1984

Dear Alan,

You might be interested to know another bod is collecting material for a BF biography. Advertises in Lamp of Thoth as follows: 'A.C. Highfield has embarked upon a biography of Dion Fortune, and has come up against obstructionism by the old occult Establishment.' Is there something about Fortune that somebody doesn't want us all to know? Highfield therefore asks LOT readers for help in personal reminiscences and factual documentational information.

I'm wondering why all of a sudden this rush for "telling the world" about DF? Very odd.

Afraid I can't help very much. I was very young (about 15-16) when I rather daringly went as far as Queensborough Terrace and inflicted myself. She happened to be there, but all I remember is a rather large and powerful woman who made a tremendous impression on me, <u>but</u>, at the same time made it perfectly clear that she did <u>not</u> consider teenagers were very suitable people to handle occult topics. She was perfectly nice about this, but I felt so upset about what seemed to me a personal rejection, that I was actually glad to get out of the place. Her general remarks were to the effect that <u>when</u> I'd grown a lot older and had some practical experience I would be very welcome to come back, and I remember feeling (but not saying) "Yes, but if you aren't prepared to help me achieve that development, why should you have the benefit of it when I've got it from somewhere else?" Pity I didn't say it at the time. I fancy she was wearing some kind of grey woolly jumper and skirt, was sitting at some kind of desk and fiddling with a paperknife or something of that sort. She was probably perfectly right, but I took everything very much to heart then, and was terribly sensitive for any form of what I might interpret as personal rejection. What of course I hadn't realised was that she wasn't very keen on teenagers anyway, they just weren't her favourite kind of people any more than they are mine now. But somehow, (I don't quite know how myself) that contact had forged a sort of psychic link between us, and I felt her in the background for many years later. There was a sort of "genuineness" you can feel yet not explain.

Later on I was to pick up those kinks again via Mary Gilchrist at Glastonbury who took over DF's old army hut there where Geoffrey Ashe is now. By the time I joined the Inner Light officially that old horror Arthur Chichester had taken over and they all went very Scientological, so I didn't stay very long. It just wasn't the same without DF, although it wasn't ever what you might call a friendly and human atmosphere at all. Not a warm and welcoming affair, but a sort of correct, formal, and terribly rigid sort of encounter, as one might expect with a professional accountant or solicitor. Off-putting as it were. Or that's the effect it had on me anyway. Oh yes, the notion of her dichotomy between the dual side of her nature resulting in the blood disorder which killed her is partly my own conclusion, and partly from a confidential source. Looking back, I am convinced she suffered from a lot of sex-repression due to the mores of her social structure, as witness those two books; "Problem of Purity", and "Love and Marriage". Why else might she book those appointments with a Freudian psychoanalyst just before she died?

I shall greatly look forward to reading your mythography of her. My tribute to her of course was the Talking Tree, which I am convinced she helped me get together.

Yesterday I was up in London with Don Weiser and his wife Betty Lundsted at Watkins Bookshop which he has taken a majority shareholding in. They are a lovely couple personally and we had an enjoyable day, though I must admit that my advancing years are beginning to make these outings a lot more difficult than they once were. Don tells me that the big time for occult books is over, and what sells best now is Astrology and holistic medicine stuff, My stuff sells slowly, but continually and consistently. which in the long run is really best. I can't honestly say I've had a rush of useful respondents from anywhere, or any great enthusiasm for the Sangreal Concept at all, which is just what I expected. Only one enquiry from the UK. at all, and that vague and unimpressive. Many from California, some of whom still write me enthusiastically, one in particular, a middle aged woman whose life ambition it seems to to to be ordained as a priest - and looks like achieving it. In the USA you hand over your dollars and get your ordination certificate just like that. She amuses me, so I write occasionally.

You're working in an old folks home now??? God save me from those places. I used to visit them enough [as a chiropodist]. Still, I hope it works out OK for you. Also I hope your baby survives, though I honestly believe this is a <u>terrible</u> world to bring another soul into. I grew up with the strongest instinct never to bring any other soul into incarnation, and of course I can see now why.

I've no objection to your writing a critical analysis of my work, providing you make it perfectly plain that my entire motivation in life has been the preservation of the roots and <u>essence</u> of our Western Tradition per se, and almost desperately trying to persuade people to look for those roots in themselves. Those roots are not specifically Pagan, Christian, Druidic, Rosicrucian, or any kind of "ism" at all, but are genetic, ethnical and blood linked, hence the Sangreal Symbolism. That is "back of and behind" everything else. So once you recognise <u>that</u> you can call yourself formally with anything whatsoever if you want to, or simply stick with the basic Concept itself. The Sangreal Concept <u>is</u> the summing up of my entire life.

Hoping to go down to Glastonbury again. next week for the day with friends, and maybe might plant something on DFs grave.

Now in a bit of rush, because I've just had a bit of a flood of mail in and I don't much like writing letters. All the best to you and yours. As KQ, as we say in the Sodality.

Bill

Trowbridge Libary   12ᵗʰ March 2023

Hello Bill!
I note the first use of KQ here, which means 'Keep Questing'. I don't mean to sound curmudgeonly (something you were accused of), but I don't think it has really taken off.

I started this by typing in the garden office but it's wickedly cold so I've come down to the library, which is a short walk from where we live. Arcane, unseen but august Powers do seem to have arranged my life well in this respect. I couldn't live anywhere that doesn't have a library of actual physical books, lined up in their tens of thousands like all the dead people who might want to teach me things. Mainly I look for biographies.

You asked about the sudden rush to find out about DF, the bewildering question **Why?** What's it all about? you wonder.

It strikes me that you're like Galahad – or was it Perceval? - asking the Fisher King what was the meaning of the Wasteland. Dear oh dear oh dear… Those gallant knights were/are to my mind virulently virgin Prancing Prigs, who would rather tackle armoured demons than have gentle, loving contact with warm-hearted women and their quims. I suppose you might call those lads Incels these days, meaning Involuntary Celibates, although in my youth they would have been described as Can't Get Shagged.

But I've had a sudden **Oh!**

Ye gods…Here beneath the high glass of the atrium with hailstones smashing down, I've just realised something…As I've now been diagnosed with a Stone in my bladder that'll have to be removed when my heart gets stronger (lest the Stone kill me like the previous one nearly did), I suppose *I'm* a Fisher King - who was euphemistically described as having a 'wound in the thigh'! And the Grail being sometimes called the 'lapis exelis'. Well bollocks to that too, in a manner of speaking. When my heart is strong enough, I'll have it blasted out by ultrasound, I'm not gonna create my own Wasteland of Whining until then.

Have I shared too much again?

But you asked **Why**…? I've found that when people have shown interest in DF, or Mathers, or Moriarty or Christine Hartley, they *always* find strange personal connections, whether intellectual, familial, historical, geographical, or just via difficult-to-describe Happenstance. With DF, it's the personality that draws them, or what they imagine it to have been, as given out strongly in the wonderful *Psychic Self Defence*, and her compelling novels. I dare say that A.C. Highfield (now a cherished 'friend' of mine on Facebook) could probably do his own story about the connections *he* found with respect to DF and the Spirit of *his* Places. I might think of his story as being *He, himSelf and Dion Fortune*, although as I recall he could fit *Dr. Moriarty* into that story too.

I say this while the storm outside increases, and as if by magick I have an email from Rebsie Fairholm, Basil Wilby's daughter and founder of Skylight Press. This reads in part....

> It's odd, I had a sense of Bill Gray's presence around yesterday, for no apparent reason. I hope he hasn't come to kick my arse for publishing things about him after his death...
>
> Life does have a habit of lining things up in weird ways, and one of mine is that I've now played two music performances in a gig venue [next door] at 16 Bennington Street. I stood on the stage thinking about the history of the Western Mystery Tradition which unfolded on the other side of the wall, and thought about Dad attending Bill's discussion evenings, and how he must have sat near that same wall without any idea that in sixty years' time his then-unborn daughter would be playing a gig on the other side of it. It's just as well Bill doesn't still live there, or he'd be disgusted by the fucking racket coming through the wall. No.14 is now a poncy interior design studio, after many years as a cake shop. I don't think he'd like it.

Your phrase about DF and 'sex repression'... The original Grail Winners would have known all about that before they buggered off to their shiny heavens and left the rest of us to rot. But in DF's time her whole society suffered. The best medical knowledge at the time warned that masturbation (known then as 'self abuse') caused huge damage on every level – physical emotional, mental and spiritual. Look at the wonderful magus W.B. Yeats, who spent years gasping for a shag from Maude Gonne, and who made guilty comments in his Magical Diary when he had to relieve himself after months of torment.

And DF herself.... I am certain she was epileptic – hence all the physical turbulence in *Psychic Self Defence* that she described as a psychic attack (perhaps by Annie Horniman?). They were grand mals, Bill. They believed in those days that epilepsy was caused by masturbation, and the recommended 'cure' was doses of bromide. As an old soldier you'll recall that they used to put this in squaddies' tea in the olden days, to stop them getting too horny and thus not fit for fighting.

Oh but your 'Talking Tree'! Dense, and sometimes difficult to read, but a work of genius. You told me that Bobbie inspired it: 'Why do we need bloody Hebrew, eh?' And then the spirit of DF took you over as you 'brought through' her ideas, sometimes in full trance. I did an essay called '22 Shades of Gray' championing your Tarot Correspondences that the SIL put in the excellent (though now defunct) Journal, even though they didn't agree.

Why...? As a teenager, before I ever contacted you, I wrote to the Warden of the SIL and asked for any biographical details of this 'Dion Fortune'. The Warden then, John Makin, wrote back that the Personality is completely unimportant, and that the Teachings were what I should be absorbing. To me then, as now, the Personality is *all* important, as it provides the vehicle, the glamour, the mystique that makes mere philosophies come alive.

I probably would have liked Makin for one odd reason...

Makin had no idea who the man was issuing his books at his local library. This was the late and lovely Peter Larkworthy, who was covertly a power behind the scenes of the Wiccan movement. Peter, who was one of the Real Ones, told me that Makin's books were all Westerns.

Oh and one final thing... You commented that this is a 'terrible world to bring another soul into'. I remember how you and Bobbie could never understand why Murry Hope was so desperate to have a baby (she never did). But you and Bobbie were almost exactly the same age as my parents. I personally think, looking back, that I was born into the most perfect of eras, all things considered. My wife and I have both had strange and adventuresome lives, not always happy or easy, but we agree that we have experienced the Last of the Best and the Best of the Last. I'm not saying that I'm the child you never had, because I feel no filial connection at all. I'm just suggesting that you might have got that one wrong.

Storm outside and library closing soon.... There's a *very* elderly man wearing the same overcoat as me and the same Poundshop spectacles who seems to want to talk to me...

                    Take care

alan

And as I say to the cognoscenti...
HWTL

Wm. G. Gray
14. Bennington St.
Cheltenham
Glos. GL50 4ED

Telephone

(0242) 24129

23 SEP 1984

Dear Alan,

While I was away visiting old friends recently, I came across a small bit of information concerning Dion Fortune which was unknown to me and sufficiently amusing to pass along to you. The only thing is that I cdn't guarantee it nor authenticate it, nor even give you names of my source. All I can tell you is that it came to me from someone who was once connected with the Inner Light. The information itself concerns the origins of her nickname "Fluff".

It seems that this derived entirely from her household habit of checking the cleanliness of rooms by the time-honoured way of running a finger along suspicious surfaces and then if any dirt appeared on its end presenting it accusingly at whoever she thought guilty, exclaiming firmly "Look! that's fluff!" She'd do this so regularly and frequently the word stuck to her in the end...

While on my visit I came across an extraordinary village church at a place in Dorset called Whitchurch Canonicorum. Extraordinary because it is the only one in the entire UK (unless you except Westminster Abbey) which still has the intact shrine of its original "Saint", and which is still in use. As you know, all such shrines were destroyed at the Reformation as being "superstitious", and the bones were hurled in all directions. Edwards were left in Westminster because he was a King. The exact reason for this Dorsetshire "Saint" being left intact were not given, but the probability was that she was a local woman, and therefore it only counted as a tomb.

Almost nothing is actually known about St Wite, except that she was a Saxon woman of middle age who was murdered by a raiding Danish band, of marauders, So were many others, but why her bones in particular were revered is still a mystery. The fact is that they are still there in a lead casket in this altar-type tomb in the village church, with three large "vesica pisces" cavities beneath the thick slab, before which one knelt, pushed ones head through the hole and prayed aloud for ones petition to be granted. The thick stone separators prevented one being heard by the other petitioner kneeling a couple of feet away in a similar position. The cavities also served as collecting places for offerings. There are still kneeling pads (modern) in front of the holes which reminded me of modern plastic telephone hoods.

The holes were crammed with cards on which messages were written. There must have been several hundreds. Loose money is still left in them which is collected and given to various charities. On a nearby altar is a note-book and pencil with which odd petitions may be written. some of than were heartbreaking, one of them in particular written in a childish hand was: "Dear God, please cure my mum of cancer." The evidence of such faith in modern times was simply <u>intense</u>. I can't think of a more suitable word.

"Saint" Wite herself may have been no more than a Saxon housewife of the 8th century who got in the way of a gang of murderous muggers who killed her for fun, but her bones are still speaking in this century with very great effect. Of course the term "Saint" was very loosely used in her times and usually meant no more than being a reputedly good person. Wite is certainly not in any Calender or recognised outside her own village in our times, but she certainly spoke loudly enough to me. It is nice to find such a splendid anachronism in our times...

I couldn't get near to the Cerne Abbas giant for a <u>good</u> picture, but those I did have come out well enough.

A curiosity on the outer walls of St Wite's church was a carving thought to represent the Holy Grail. It was a <u>two-handled</u> vessel said to be in common use in local English churches as a communion cup in former times. Of course we know that a chalice-form Cup didn't get used till the 6th century in Celtic churches, and the earliest ones were ones were made from pottery, glass, wood, etc, and often bowl-shaped in design. Hence the famous bit of the Nanteos Cup <u>could</u> have been a very early Celtic communion Cup. I've actually held the thing in my hands. But I've never visualised or even heard of a two-handled Cup, especially one with a narrowish neck such as on shown in the carving. It reminded me of the vessel shown in the "Arms of Joseph of Aramathea" to be seen at Glastonbury, where there are<u> two</u> such vessels one on each side of a "ragged Cross", one said to hold the blood. and the other the sweat (or seed) taken from the body at the Crucifixion. True, the handled vessel would enable the thing to be passed from one communicant to another without much risk of spilling the contents, but somehow it doesn't seem appropriate. Jewish "Kiddush Cups" were made of silver, and something like a modern tumbler or ancient beaker in shape; You can still buy them in Jewish religious supply shops. They haven't changed in several millennia.

I still keep getting odd letters from America mostly concerning the Sangreal, but only two from this country and neither of any interest. My South African friend tells me that he is virtually recovered and hopes to see me in January. This will probably be about the last time in this incarnation I can make such a journey, so I'm just hoping for the best.

The road outside my place is still in a hell of a mess and God knows when it will be finished. Otherwise I'm still pottering along waiting for my next book to be published and wondering what else to write if anything. It certainly doesn't look as if that bit of plant I took from DF's grave is going to grow. Incidentally, I heard that she was buried close to Loveday, but I never checked the near-by graves. Not the same Loveday as Crowley's by the way. I wonder why she wasn't cremated? She could still have had her ashes scattered in the Tor.

That's about all at the moment. I thought I'd send on that bit of Fluff while it was still fresh in my mind. Hope all is going well with you.

Bill

Cafe #1   14th March 2023

Dear…? *Who?*

I am… gently startled and a bit humbled after that last letter – the latter not being one of my usual states.

Where was the legendary **William G. Gray** – whom you once self-described as the oldest 'Angry Young Man' in the business? You know who I mean… the toddler who had been dandled on Crowley's knee (perhaps your biological father? - as I've often wondered but was afraid to ask); the teen with bum-fluff on upper lip who prised Dion Fortune from her den; the young squaddy who had sneaked into the Great Pyramid when he shouldn't; the veteran subaltern who had been machine-gunned and bombed at Dunkirk and who wrestled with his PTSD (unknown at the time!) in his own way; who had secret involvement in Military Intelligence; the Honoured Stranger whom the Arch-Druid invited to the Stonehenge ceremonies; the man who worked magick with the Witches and lambasted the scary Warden of the SIL; who went on to write about Magic and the Kabbalah with a clarity and depth that few have equalled before and many have stolen from since. There are many witches and wizards 'out there' today implying that their teachings have been handed down from the depths of the Wildwood or ancient Magical Lodges, but in fact they came from 14 Bennington Street, GL50 4ED.

In this *lovely* letter I hear you for the first time as 'Bill'! Maybe that's my own fault. Physically, I am hearing impaired and becoming more so. Perhaps I have been 'hearing impaired' on personal or even spiritual levels too? It showed you as you are, and perhaps always was. Someone once said (It was David Bowie actually) that when you get old, you become the person you always were. I hope that now I'm your age, I can become a better Alan.

I used your yarn about The Fluff as the opening to my *Dancers to the Gods* – a most unsatisfying book as I see it now. But the rest of it was *completely* new to me. I have a deep passion for Dorset, and always feel somewhat buzzy when I'm there, crossing into it from the southern border from Wiltshire. I always ask permission of Place when entering other territories.

I have actually been to Whitchurch Canonicorum. That was in 2001, after my second marriage ended, and I toured the county with a part-time girlfriend. We were both more attracted to Dorset than we were to each other. She had the address of a B&B and we came to a large rather splendid house with quite lovely rooms. The door was open yet there was no-one there. Nor in the large but whispering garden. On a bookshelf in the lounge there were numerous New Agey books, including DF's *The Mystical Qabalah* – although, hold on, I might be creating a false memory there. I do that easily. Which is why I never put any faith in hypnotic regressions, especially anything to do with aliens or past lives – including my own. But there was an *otherness* about the whole place, a *tone* about the whole area in fact, as you seemed to notice. It made me recall the many stories of people stepping into parallel worlds – often hotels in remote countryside – that later proved non-existent in this Time and Space. No-one appeared, so we made our excuses to the pulsing emptiness and left.

I didn't get to the church. I was still in too much of a 'turbulent priest' mode after the breakdown of my marriage to Michelle. Yet my ears, for all their physical hearing problems, pricked up when I read about St. Wite!

Shamefully, despite me being a Dorset Bore, I'd never heard of her even though she is the Patron Saint of the county, whose feast day is June 1st. I'll make sure I remember that. She was Latinised by the Catholic Church into being Saint *Candida*. Trust that rotten lot to choose a name that evokes to the modern mind all those vaginal infections that anyone can all get. (I remember when the late Laura Jennings, the hierophant of a Golden Dawn Temple in the US, visited us in Limpley Stoke, she confessed to having troublesome candida - 'thrush' – and was trying to ease it by natural, holistic means. Because she imagined that I was a spiritual, farseeing sort of chappy, when I told her to go to the local chemist in Bradford on Avon and buy a tube of Canesten for 50 pence and use it, she did so, and it cured her.)

So back to the delightful and healthily named St. **Wite...**

She may have been of Breton origin but no-one really knows. She seems to have protected her people from all sorts of harm. 'Wite' is described as an Old English word that may mean sage or wise man – but never wise *woman*.

I can almost hear you bristling now Bill! Everyone who ever met you was given long lectures about the word 'wicca', supposedly meaning Wise. You hated the term. *Wicca wicca wicca...*

I like those old Saints who have little or no historical substance. My personal favourite is Saint Katherine – she of the Wheel – who was/is patron of my local area in particular. I wrote at some length about her in my *Searching for Sulis* that you may have enjoyed.

But I think that 'Katherine' is a construct, perhaps like an icon on a touchscreen that can be used to open up whole realms. In my case going back to Neolithic times and beyond, surviving – thriving – via tribal DNA, as I think I said earlier. And so I suspect that *all* the Saints/Guides/Masters/ Chancellors and the rest have something of this nature and function. You taught me something like that in the 1960s, as I recall, though of course DNA hadn't been invented then.

Apropos of nothing, I wish I could send you the book *The Masters Revealed* by K. Paul Johnson. In it he shows that the Theosophical Masters were neither disembodied spirits nor fictions, but actual historical personages. Their identities at the time were disguised for various political reasons, and Blavastky rather naughtily added a certain amount of what we would now call spin. I say this because I've just seen on-line, via my phone, someone talking about the awesome 'Master Kuthumi' from that of the excruciating group known as the Great White Brotherhood. Am I the only man alive who remembers that H.P. Blavatsky herself always described him as Koot Hoomi lal Singh? His real name, according to Johnson, was 'Sirdar Thakar Singh Sandhanwalia', founder of the 'Singh Sabha', whose aim was to reform Sikhism and bring back into the fold the apostates who had converted to other religions; as well as to interest the British officials in furthering the Sikh community. All part of the 'Great Game' between Russian and British colonial forces in which HPB herself was fully involved. When HPB described meeting KH in Hyde Park it wasn't because he had teleported himself from the Himalayas, but more likely because he had a meeting with the bods at the Foreign Office in King Charles Street, to state his case.

I babble again. I must try and persuade Margaret, my third wife and first soul-mate, to visit the church in Dorset, where we'll say a prayer for you and Bobbie, just in case you're both reincarnated again, in America, as Marcia said...

Alan

Wm. G. Gray
14. Bennington St.
Cheltenham
Glos. GL50 4ED

Telephone

(0242) 24129

22 June 1984

Dear Allan,

Many thanks for your latest with interesting news. Sorry to hear of Christine Hartley's collapse, but she must be a hell of an age and anyone is entitled to go then. So long as it is merciful, that is the main thing. It isn't that one dies that is the worry, but how it happens. The Chinese have a saying that there is only one gate into incarnation but a thousand out of it, and there are probably a lot more than that.

    I didn't actually know where DF's private Temple was, or the comic lift. I would have given her credit for more sense than that, but she had a right to play with the toys she paid for, and you have to remember the deus ex machine bit, plus the fact that <u>all</u> our most ancient attempts at relationship with "The Gods" derived from the dramatic instinct in humanity. Deity and drama are inseparable. Impossible to tell which came first, <u>probably</u> a sense of Deity with drama as an almost immediate response, but they certainly go together like opposite ends of the same stick.

    I've only a few days back mailed off my latest effusion to Weisers by ordinary sea mail. Since it wont see the light of day for at least a couple of years, what's the hurry? The Tarot book got taken, and. that'll be another year or more. I'm looking forward to your book with a lot of interest.

    When you come to think of it, the <u>real</u> "occult books" of today are not written <u>as</u> occult books. They may be psychological, scientific, or even pure fiction with an unsuspected core of solid spiritual truth. Anything <u>except</u> an "occult" label. Clever. Still, we've seen so many of our old myths suddenly solidify and start breathing heavily down our necks. All the medieval magicians who dreamed of calling up the Devil, and what else is nuclear fission '? The flying carpets that one now queues up for at airports? The seven leagued boots one keeps in a garage? BUT, would any of them have materialised without the IDEA that entered human heads so long ago and took centuries to find their way out of human fingers???? All the others will arrive in their time. The Elixir of Life. The Universal Panacea. Just materialised Consciousness, but <u>when</u> are we to find our materials spiritualised? The process has to be reversible, or rather <u>cyclical</u>, since a circle is always going in opposite directions at the same time.

It is a bit ironic to think of DF's ideology transferred to India, but do remember she wasn't so much anti-oriental as pro-occidental. It just seemed to her that no one was standing up for the West, and that was what she would do. She just saw the unbalance and tried to correct it a little. On the other hand you have to remember all the Christian missionaries of opposing opinions that we inflicted on the Orientals - and the Africans too, mostly in the 19th century. So the oriental invasion of our thought territory was only a tit for a tat really. And you should also bear in mind the political angle, plus the commercial bid. I'm not at all sure that the commercial angle exported from America wasn't worse than all the subtle sneakiness of the Russo-Indian influence of Blavatsky and her "Masters".

The thing was that we did not have a pure native Inner Tradition. Even the Druids were not native per se, but an hereditary priesthood attached to the invading Celts much as the Brahmins were with the Indo-Aryans of the Indian continent, and probably connected with them quite closely. A pity they were so opposed to literary records, though their insistence on an oral Tradition has most likely impressed it into our genes a lot more deeply than we suppose.

Why there should have been such a fascination with early Egyptian symbology and esotericism during the last century I'm not sure at all, unless it was the fact that so much was being retrieved just then, plus the medieval Trismegistic suppositions. Mostly the so-called Hermetic Doctrines which lay behind a lot of the Gnostic beliefs which had survived to a considerable extent. That is to say it was <u>available</u> – at least to scholars who made translations possible. The accuracy of such translations is always in question, and so too is the accuracy of individual reactions with them. The sense does not lie so much in an actual word, but in the readers or hearers comprehension of it. A written or spoken phrase which does not have a great effect on one individual may open up a whole flood of awareness in another. So with symbols, or tones of voice. It was a question of knowing which did what.

So the esotericism of the last century which DF would encounter was very tinged with Egyptian and of course Hebraic, philosophy, neither of which were truly integral to this country (or indeed Europe) except by adoption. No one knew (or yet does) exactly how the Egyptians pronounced their language, and only educated guesses are made by comparisons with Coptic and Hebrew which still survive, as does Amharic. The chances are that our esoteric origins were much as the rest of the world classed under the generic heading of Shamanisn, or plain Nature worship as interpreted by individuals and passed down a long line of descendants each making their own contribution until something standard or settled arose out of it all. As for example what is happening with Voodoo at present. It is becoming quite a sophisticated religion based on rather tribal spiritualism, but it is <u>not</u> specifically African in the least, and I gather there are quite a few White members.

Of course DF was entirely hooked on the Atlantis myth as so many still are, although the so-called "Lost Continent" may well be founded in <u>genetic memories</u> of another world altogether. The idea per se is a good or encouraging one, because it provides both a built-in impetus and a salutory warning. Translated fundamentally, Atlantis makes a valuable myth, but taken literally it hasn't much to offer. DF <u>was</u> inclined to take interpretations too literally very often.

I'm interested that someone in India is claiming to be in touch with the defunct DF. I wonder what sort of "messages" are being passed? And thanks, I would like a copy of any picture including her. I'm shoving one of me in regalia into this one, since I had a few taken for the Brazilians who kept enquiring about robes for the Sangreal Sacrament. Don't publish it till after I'm dead. Also don't bother to try a mythography of me, I do assure you there isn't anything which would make any sort of a story.

Anyhow I do hope your life takes a turn for the more satisfactory, and I will continue to keep you in my thoughts and prayers.

                        Fraternally,

                        Bill

Trowbridge Library   15th March 2023

Dear Bill,

How odd. I always take a single letter from the Second Tranche and reply accordingly, without sneaking a look at the one that follows. Yet it seems from your comments about the "subtle sneakiness of the Russo-Indian influence of Blavatsky and her Masters", that you pre-empted me. *Logically*, your letter of the 22nd June 1984 must have lodged in my subconscious, hence my own apparently spontaneous 'Apropos of nothing' was simply an upsurge of remembering. Or, *Illogically*, but far more interesting, there were all sorts of 'timey wimey things going on (I'm homaging David Tennant's *Dr. Who* with that description). So... perhaps your 71½ self was somehow writing to my own 71½ self at the same moment?

Again, almost all of your letter was completely new to me. 'DF's ideology being transferred to India?' Eh? No idea! But I half-heartedly agree with you about the Atlantis myth – if that's what it is. Yes, it was very important to DF and Christine Hartley and Kim Seymour and many others at the time. To them, the Lost Continent was probably somewhere in the South Atlantic. I've read dozens of books arguing (each of them persuasively) that it was in… Antarctica, before the Earth's crust shifted and it froze; a memory of Crete and/or Thera; Doggerland; Bimini; the very North Atlantic where it was the original of Thule; and now there's the argument that it was actually in the Sahara!

Gareth Knight took the traditional approach and I was at one of the Hawkwood 'do's' and saw him in full (and I must say awesome) flow when he summoned up all manner of energies and entities.

Plus there have been places in the West Country (Brean and Weston super Mare) where I've been almost overwhelmed by a tidal waves of energies of such incredible age then I can only use the word 'Atlantean' to describe them. When I took Dolores to meet Christine Hartley at her retirement flat in Winchester, they both instantly 'recognised' each other from specific Atlantean times.

So who am I to say that it was 'just a myth'.

(And yet, as I scribble this, two emails have just arrived, one inviting me to an 'Atlantis Workshop', and the other from the legendary Atlantis Bookshop in London.)

While it seems to be fully explorable on another dimension, I rather like the idea that it might actually have existed on 'another world altogether'. Mars, perhaps? as you once suggested to me. I always felt (or rather hoped) that you knew more about this than you were willing to reveal. Odd, too, that I've had recent correspondence from someone working in the JPL Labs in California telling me things I cannot yet write about that but which are blisteringly relevant to what I've just said. He's offered to show me around these labs if we ever go to California (we won't); I've offered to show him around the Limpley Stoke Valley, which is the setting of my novel *The Moonchild*, my homage to the Crowley original. To give context, 'JP' stands for Jack Parsons – Crowley's marvellous follower and rocket pioneer. And the Limpley Stoke Valley is the nexus of all things to do with Dion Fortune – and mySelf.

Place place place – Spirit of Place! Far healthier and more potent than anything else I know. Someone (probably me) once wrote that when you become aware of the Gods, they become aware of you. And I will argue that that is true of Spirit of Place.

Yes, Christine Hartley had a heart attack. I went to visit her in hospital in Winchester. I parked near the gates of King Alfred's College, which is grandly entitled, but was simply one of the myriad of 'teacher training colleges' that you could get into without many qualifications. If I'd gone to KAC in Winchester in the South West of England, where I was inexplicably desperate to go, instead of the North Counties College in the North East of England, my life would have taken a differing path. I think. I'd have linked with W.E. Butler, with whom I'd been corresponding before I tracked you down, Bill. And my magick would have taken a very different tone. I think. Outside the gates of KAC it was as though I had stepped into the current of a Parallel Life, I felt twisted and turned on profound inner levels[1].

'Fascination with Egypt' you ponder... I had no interest in Egypt. Then at a Spiritualist Church in Bath the tiny medium, a certain Mrs Butler from Weston super Mare (probably no relation to WEB) told me that I was connected with a big black dog, with very point ears. And that in some sense it *was* me.

---

1   See my collection of essays *Short Circuits*, self-published on Amazon

Bollocks, I thought, smiling blankly at this eruption of astral junk. But then a week later on Battersea Common I met Dolores, and got the first whisperings of the name Anubis, about Whom I knew nothing.

And now as I write here in the Atrium, bugger me (but please not literally), a fellow who was an SIL initiate has just strolled past. He's a nice lad, whose garden abuts ours. And also a chap who was once the High Priest of Peter Larkworthy's coven! There's a lot of 'us' around in the small area we inhabit though we never socialise. Me, I don't like meeting people because they want to talk about Magicks, but when I indulge I always feel a bit 'dirty' afterward. Don't ask me to explain. Maybe it's my own inner sense of 'phoneyness' that causes that.

We'd never get on today in person, Bill.

I'm not the chatty type, and you know fuck all about football.

I don't think you'd quite 'get' me.

alan

Wm. G. Gray
14. Bennington St.
Cheltenham
Glos. GL50 4ED

Telephone

(0242) 24129

4 DEC 1984

Dear Alan

Thanks for your recent letter with its very graphic description of the Sangreal Sodality in your own words out of your own thoughts. That's exactly what it is. We aren't talking about two different things, but simply describing the same idea out of two different minds. So what? All I've done is link it with a spiritually genetic factor which I see as the Sangreal principle because of its b1ood significance. Nothing more or less. So what do you propose doing about it?

As one might expect, I've no response from this country worth considering, but they've got a Sangreal Group going in Florida to my knowledge, and they've actually built a special Temple in Brazil as well as South Africa. Unless I drop dead shortly or something more serious happens, I should be going to South Africa next month until about the middle of February. I've also been invited to Florida, but am not in the least keen on the USA. Their Group leader has promised to come over next year and meet with me anyway but one never knows with Americans. They're all over you with superlatives one second, and the next they don't even know who the hell you are. In other words it's all surface and no depth. That's why I prefer South Africans. They're much more like us. If they like you they really mean it.

All I've actually done in fact is suggest some structure to the Sangreal Concept, and if anybody doesn't like it they are at perfect liberty to work out their own and get it going as best they can. Maybe I should have thrown in a few group-gropes or mutual masturbation sessions or whatever eccentricities the kids are getting up to in lieu of serious spiritual work these days. Eventually they'll be afraid of any kind of straightforward sex because of AIDS, so they'll have to invent substitutes for satisfaction, and the imagination boggles at possibilities!!!

I wish I could say congratulations on your forthcoming child, but in view of the world situation and its prospects I honestly can't congratulate <u>anybody</u> for getting themselves born into this muck-heap. Somehow I can sympathise with the Quaker idea of a naming ceremony which they hold in place of baptism. Apparently they simply hold the baby up in the presence of several Friends and someone says out loud "...(Name)...... We welcome thee to this vale of tears." - and that's it. Not a bad concept. I could think of similar ceremonies where the general idea is to commiserate with the incoming soul, pray for his/her ability to perform whatever the appointed task might be, and then hope for a happy death at the end of it and freedom from obligation to return. I'm not in the least looking forward to my next incarnation. In fact I'm rather dreading it, but the work has to go on, and as Jawn Wayne is reputed to have said; "A man's gotta do what a man's gotta, do-oo."

Anyhow, I hope you manage to get that cottage you want and continue to prosper. Perhaps some time next year I might manage to drift over for a few words. Don't depend on it though. When is your mythography of Dion Fortune going to be done? I think that was a really great idea. Several up and coming authors seem to have the same idea in mind, so you would be well advised to get your blow in first…

Doesn't it strike you as a bit odd that so many people are getting the same fundamental ideas on the Sangreal but expressed in different forms? Jung's postulations concerning the Universal Subconsciousness seem certainly correct and they tie in with his synchronicity ideas as well…

Oh well, maybe we shall meet later next year…
All the best and KQ

Bill

Town Hall Cafe   11th March 2023

Dear Bill,
I'm scribbling this in the Town Hall caff: a town that is, as I've long argued using the sort of etymological dictionary that you treasured, named after Trolls. The new owners of the cafe are Chinese, from Hong Kong. *My first wife was Chinese and I lived in Hong Kong!* I said brightly. I might now be their favourite customer. They even knew *Tin Hau Temple Road*, though none of them had ever met my ex father-in-law, Dr. Ou – who was taller than me and looked like Gregory Peck.

Hmmm… 'graphic description of the Sangreal Sodality' you write. I do remember parts of that letter. But I disagree, I still can't make a connection between that channelled input that seemed to come to me from DF, and your Sangreal. Mine was to do with what we now call 'group souls", I suppose, but I pitched it in terms of an inner tribal thing. I called it the *Microcosmic Doctrine*, tongue-in-cheekly. What did I do about it, you ask? I put it in several of my later books where it seemed relevant but I didn't *do* anything. Even now, when the *Mic. Doc.* seems to explain things about my inner life, I don't ***Do***, I just ***Be***. And so the oddest and inspirational things – happenstances, serendipities and synchronicities flow into my life from outer levels. I don't have visions, as you had of the Sangreal that was almost tangible; yet unexpected, weird and often absurd encounters seem to happen on an almost daily basis.

A Sangreal group leader from Florida? I wonder if that was Laura Jennings, before she moved to Seattle? I'm sure she did come and visit you once in Cheltenham. Her group when I knew her was pure Golden Dawn. The Ra-Horakhte Temple or something. I liked her very much but we fell out regularly. She was hugely wise yet strangely naive and seem to see us English as under-functioning versions of Americans. To me the GD system was *also* behind its time, despite the glamour of it in American eyes in particular. I've got a group photo of them all robed, wearing nemysses. Are there any functioning GD groups in the UK today?

But Bill, I'm going to get pissy with you after the tone of your comment about the 'forthcoming child'. Tomorrow we will take said child for a meal at a riverside restaurant in Bradford on Avon, not far from the Thomas More church. Her name is Zoë, which means *Life*, of course, and she is 38 now. She will tell you herself that despite the normal slings and arrows of exasperations caused by irritating parents, she has had and *will continue to have* a wonderful life. More than that – do shut up and listen Bill! – she and her husband adopted three little boys, siblings, aged 1½ to 5, taking them from the darkness and torments of their appalling 'biological' parents and gave them Wonders, persisting with Love through the hugely difficult first year when it was scary for all of them. Slowly, we've seen them grow into boys who are themselves now trusting, kind, thoughtful and cuddly. They give 'Magic Grandad and Magic Granny' (*aka* me and Margaret) love that *you* have never known. In the debate about Nature or Nurture, then Nurture wins every time as far as we are concerned. These little boys are loved every bit as much, and feel as close to us, as the five 'biological' grandchildren from my other daughters.

What have *you* brought into the world that could begin to compare? What goodness, kindness and selflessness has ever bubbled from the bowl of the Sangreal? To me, it's a spiritualised piece of Tupperware. And I can say that now without fear because I know how it's going to end with you, and that it caused you nothing but disappointment.

Hmmm...

It's pouring down outside now. I'll make it stop soon.

But I'm *still* a bit tetchy, and I'm no longer afraid of you.

Listen... in my mid-teens I learned to astrally project and look down at my own body for the first time and tell myself that I'm not as ugly as I'd thought; I raised the kundalini in that same year and communed with my future self; I went to the High Place of the Moon in cahoots with FPD before I'd even shaved; I've had endless sagas of what seems to be group reincarnation involving Benedictine monks and also Templars; I've raised 'Atlantean' energies from a grave in Dorset when invoking the spirit of Lord Eldon; I've strolled alongside the River Wansbeck with my sister on one side and the wizard Michael Scot on the other, both chatting away on differing levels; I've exorcised low-grade Beings and sometimes self-exorcised myself; I *know* the feeling of the Land and its Peoples soaking up through my feet; I've even had two meetings with an Extra-Terrestrial who seems to like me! Oh yes and regular glimpses of Yeshua (a nice lad, though certainly no Son of God), and his lass.

But despite all these (and *many* more), NOTHING has compared to the bliss of being called **Dad.** No joy in my life has been purer or more holy than tucking them into bed at night, making them all safe and warm, and reading them stories and 'doing the voices'.

Bill Bill Bill… despite the awe of what you felt when you had a Vision of the Grail so intense and solid you felt you could touch it, that means nothing to me. At risk of troubling you now ahead of your years to come (that I've already experienced for you), that Vision really didn't do you much good in the end, or bring you to Perfect Peace Profound as you lay strapped into your hospital bed to stop you trying to kill yourself. Stuff that into the plastic bowl of your Sangreal and see what *you* might **do** with it...

alan

Wm. G. Gray
14. Bennington St.
Cheltenham
Glos. GL50 4ED

Telephone

(0242) 24129

Walpurgis 1985

Dear Alan

Thanks a lot for galleys of "Dancers to the Gods", and best of luck with your forthcoming Dion Fortune work. I shall really look forward to reading.

I found D to the G rather nostalgic and also slightly sad. it was really a revealing account of spiritual sex between two private people. beautiful, but you first get the feeling that you shouldn't be watching their personal paradise, and then you begin to realise that in fact everyone should be sharing a Supreme Sex Act in which ALL are partakers who are not outsiders. Common Union in fact.

I do feel that the book ended a bit abruptly, and you should have said a few words at the end.

It might interest you to know (though a bit late now,) that the missing word on page 129 was undoubtedly "Consolamentum" which as you may know was the phrase used by Cathars to each other on their death-beds or in extremis. It was supposed to ensure salvation and eternal enjoyment of God. No one I know has ever been certain what it was, and there have hem many guesses, probably none of them accurate. Whatever it was, it could certainly be given very briefly. Thus it resembles the "Grail Secret" which had to be passed on before death to a worthy recipient, or ones soul could not rest in peace. Again that was only a few words which reputedly could be written on the palm of one hand.

Glad to hear your family is bearing up and you like your new home. I have the address safely. How close to Bath is it? Bob Stewart is still living in that area somewhere, and I believe the dreaded Anne Slowgrove (Marian Green) is living in his old flat now. Don't ever trust anything she says if you ever meet her. She is a pathological liar in all directions. How her nice parents could ever have had such a loathsome child has always been a mystery. I saw her running her show at the "Prediction" Festival in London recently. Do you ever go to those "dos"? Amusing really. All the fakes in creation flogging the most fearsome rubbish you ever hard of.

One wicked old so and so with a display of sticks and thorns picked from hedgerows and retailing at enormous expense to idiots and suckers, had about what I thought the prize item of fooltraps. Believe this or not. They were "exorcism tablets". Five to a tiny packet. What you were supposed to do was place them in the form of a pentagram on top of your electricity meter which would then waft their demon-destroying properties all over the house thus freeing you and yours from every evil influence.

What they were in fact, were live ordinary charcoal tablets such as you can buy in any reasonable Health shop for maybe a couple of quid a thousand. They're supposed to absorb noxious toxins in the stomach. At £2.50 for five, work out the profit. Mind you I never saw anyone actually <u>buying</u> them.

Its really that sort of thing that gets occultism a bad name, although it couldn't be worse than the Christian Church for money grabbing through the centuries. Any organised religion for that matter. Nowadays one gets used to seeing lapel labels and car stickers advertising "Born-Again Pagan"! which really started as a joke on Born Again Christians who are getting a bad name all around the world for lack of consideration to others, anti-social behaviour, and other undesirable traits, especially that of "holier than thouness". There are plenty in South Africa, where they use the old Sign oi the Fish for identification. Nobody I know there likes them. Even other Christians. These are a breed of their own.

I haven't heard from Carr Collins or anyone else out there for quite a while. And I really haven't a clue when my next book is coming out or indeed if it is coming out, though I have had advanced royalties, and acknowledgements that it should be coming out this summer, though I've got past believing this. Incidentally, I had a useless royalty cheque, (no signature) sent me twice... Never happened before. I'm told this is a not uncommon trick among publishers, and only means they just haven't enough cash in that account to cover the sum, and the delay gives them time to get the cash in. They get lavish with apologies of course. So watch out for that. First time Weisers have ever tried such a trick on me, but I'll be watching for it in future. The delay has probably cost me a fair amount owing to pound-dollar exchange. But that won't affect you.

Did I tell you old Frank Regardie was dead? Fell dead in his soup March 11th when dining with friends. Probably didn't even know he had died, and if he had of done would probably have cursed because of a missed meal. What with old Gerald Gardner going in the marmalade, and Francis in the soup, it only needs me to slide into the shit one day, and that will be that. He wanted to go with a heart attack anyway, so he got his wish. I'd always wanted to drift off peacefully in a garden on a nice warm summer afternoon preferably <u>after</u> tea. Hm, as the Hebrews say: "I should be so lucky."

I'm working on a bit of a weird book at the moment called the Bloodmother. Doubt if it'll get taken by anyone. At least I've out-written Dion Fortune.

Do you know, I keep thinking over those records of earlier "magical" workings, (if you could call them magical, which is doubtful) and they do spell a story of their own which is a roman de clef of a very curious sort. Nowadays I doubt if this could happen because the humans concerned would have simply screwed, enjoyed it, and never have had the slightest spiritual experience about any of it. Whether they actually <u>accomplished</u> anything by any of it is very problematical. In fact they were both such nice people, it may not even have occurred to them what they were doing deep down, though I think they might have suspected on those levels but wouldn't have dreamed of discussing it openly.

One day someone will get round to writing a book on sexual inhibitions of the last century (and early this one because I remember a few) which will seem highly hilarious, if not unbelievable, Plus a few errors by modems who misinterpreted meanings. For example that "legs" were unmentionable before "respectable" women, and canvas covers were made to conceal the lewd objects. <u>Never!</u> Facts were that such covers were indeed made and fitted to very expensive French-polished furniture to prevent damage or scratching by children's feet or maids brooms. No other reason, and the rest is pure fantasy by subsequent authors. Actually the US of A was responsible for a lot of oddities, such as you must never say "breast" of anything, but "bosom" was respectable. Plus it was they that started fitting bogs in the bathroom so that you always asked for a bathroom and never a more honest "house of easement", or the more ridiculous "toilet" which only means a small towel anyway. Only countryfolk would ask for an "outhouse".

At any rate thanks again, and I look forward to your masterpiece on Dion Fortune. You have a' nice easy style of writing, and don't ever try and elaborate on it. It's fine as it is. Now may I wish you and yours all the success you well deserve, and the happiness which you have more than earned.

  God Bless, and KQ.

  Bill

Trowbridge Library Atrium   March 18th
2023

Dearest Bill

Sorry I was tetchy and somewhat aggressive in my last. It's my Prime Directive as a Dad to protect my children, whether they're still just specks in the womb or breaking the hearts of the swains who have flocked around them when they matured. They're all grown up now of course and it's been quite odd to step aside, somewhat, now that they have all got strong fellas as their First Response.

Thank you for your kind comments about my 'nice and easy style of writing'. It isn't 'easily' achieved though. Even this, scribbled on an A4 notepad will be written and rewritten and re-re-written until I get into the flow of whatever energy or entity might be nudging me, so I can 'sing the body electric' so to speak. I must look a bit intense to anyone passing. Oh and I deliberately bought a new purple notepad from from a place called The Works, as slight homage to our joint Work.

Now I must *gently* upbraid you this time about the 'wicked old so and so with a display of sticks'. This was certainly the marvellous Dusty Miller, who communes with the dryads of the trees and cajoles them – willingly – into wands (like genies in bottles), so that they can experience travel. When I gave my first talk about DF, before my biography of her came out, I wouldn't take any money but asked for one of his wands. In the event he gave me two, that we call Crow and Raven. Margaret and I agree that they are among our most treasured and honoured possessions. We could do a whole book about the extraordinary events they have been involved in or often precipitated. 'Just act as if…' was all that Dusty told me, when he handed them over.

Do I believe that our two 'sticks' are connected with dryads and enable things in odd ways? Yes. Yes I do.

(Not too long ago I was giving a talk on Faery in Glastonbury, and I asked the audience if anyone had ever met the late Dusty Miller. Only one hand at the back shot up: it was Dusty Miller.)

As to those charcoal tablets… I wasn't aware of them, and certainly wouldn't have paid money. I was tempted to cut out that piece so as not to reflect badly on Dusty, but as I sit here scribbling I actually think it's a good idea! Intent is *everything*. The most potent rituals in the world won't work if there is no serious Intent. With powerful Intent, the rituals aren't needed. Again, Murry Hope inspired that in me: 'How to Banish a room?' she asked me rhetorically, as I sat there as a young man, drooling at her beauty, unable to believe how old she was. 'Just *do* it Alan! With your mind!' So if I see any such charcoal tablets I'll give it a go.

Not that we have any trouble with evil influences, although we did have a trog at the end of the house that we seem to have inherited from an odd contact of mine from Wales, whose story I want to get some day before it's too late.

But Bill, of that ilk, what would you have made of the current fad for Dream Catchers? Laura Jennings gave me a huge one. I hadn't a clue what it was. I had no feel for the device but I gave it to a friend who was having difficult times and she *swore* that it worked for her. So I try not to knock or mock anything of that sort these days.

Oh and then there is the *feng-shui* of peoples' homes: crystals placed in appropriate locations within the house. At one time you/we might have chuckled at that too, but we've done it to our house. As have two of our daughters.

I suppose you were at the juncture between 'occultism' as you experienced it and all the glamour and glitz that seemed to explode into the world for my generation. I've sometimes sneered along with you, and felt vaguely superior among the bric-a-brac of the sort of Festivals you describe. But now I think, well, Light and Love to them all. And if you can make a bit of honest dosh without lying and manipulating people, then good luck. The real magick (and I prefer the 'k') will always seep through.

So I suppose *I'm* at the juncture where this has given way to the Social Media, if that's the right term. I do know that effective Magickal Lodges seem to have opened in cyber-space connecting and awakening and training people in different continents and time-zones without ever needing to meet physically.

So if I ever moan about blogs and vlogs and tik-tokkers and all the rest I sometimes pretend not to understand, just ignore me. I think I'm just jealous at having missed a trick or two.

Your book *The Bloodmother*. I do have a very faint memory of you mentioning this. The title is powerful, and I suspect the content is provocative. I also have an even fainter idea that it did get published though with a different title. I suppose I'll consult Dr. Google on this…

Best

Alan

Wm. G. Gray
14. Bennington St.
Cheltenham
Glos. GL50 4ED

Telephone

(0242) 24129

20 Sept 1985

Dear Alan,

A little grist for your mill I hope. I was visiting friends in Dorset last week and amongst other places visited Sherborne Abbey. In one of the transepts Geoff spotted a tile with Dion Fortune's motto on it. Then many, and there were in fact endless of them. We checked, and they turned out to be the arms of the Digby family. You know the character Kenelm Digby who was famous for fighting and inventing the Powder of Sympathy which you used for treating the weapon instead of the wound it made and that did the healing. In view of what they were putting into raw wounds in those days (c. Charles 2) the wound probably healed a lot faster without the muck.

That Digby was also a bit of an alchemist, possibly an early Rosicrucian, and was certainly one of the first members of the Royal Society which still exists as our leading British scientific body, patronised by Royalty. I did some pictures which I hope come out well enough to send later in this letter, but in any case the place is close enough for you to visit on your own. Your local library will probably have enough information in it to discover the connection between DF and Kenelm Digby, or rather the family. That has to be its origin, and it could be quite significant. The Digby memorial in Sherborne Abbey is quite impressive.

I also met up with Jon Whittaker the chiropodist at Wells who used to be in my Group and is a friend of mine. He is an interesting occult character I keep in touch with and is very keen to "get a little group together". About your age I'd say. He tells me he had a message from you fixing up contact with CH. I gave your address.

It almost does seem that DF is on her way back somehow. I'm told the Inner Light has gone terribly "Chreestian" these days and all the joy has gone completely out of it (what little was there in the first place).

And yes I did see the TV bit about Earth Magic with Bob Stewart, Anne Slowgrove who poses as Marion Green and who is a pet hate of mine, et al and wasn't much impressed except by the pagan family who went to Aran. Bob's music was delightful and the photography was good.

The Sangreal Ceremonies book is coming out shortly. I've got the latest MS with Weisers, but haven't heard if they will take it or not. Personally I doubt it. I think I've done my last book in this life

Oh Bobbie just sticks her head in to say that she's pretty sure that the Digbys, Spenser, and that crew were part of the "School of Night" lot that used to meet up periodically with Raleigh at Sherborne. They might as well have been called the Elizabethan Esoterics or Occasional Occultists. Anyway there's an interesting connection there to investigate in linkage with DF. And I'll very much look forward to reading the book when it comes out.

Just heard from Weisers, they've got my MS at an evaluator who likes my stuff, and would like to have me for dinner in London when over here next month. They also think I might like to meet Warren Kenton whose work I've always admired. So that's cheering. I gather Carr Collins just got his DF book ready for publication before he died. Fungus disease of lungs apparently, but I wasn't told which. There are several. Strange way to go. Nasty too. Probably caught on travels in East.

I pray you and family are all well and prospering. God Bless and KQ.

Bill

The Atrium, Trowbridge Library   21 March 2023

Dear Bill,
The place is chock full of people 'of a certain age'. That is, *my* age. They're all wearing waterproof coats and stout boots and are now stomping out en masse like a herd of happy wildebeests. It seems they're members of the 'University of the Third Age' Walking Group of Trowbridge. I must see what else the U3A offers, though I don't think I've got anything relevant to offer during my own Third Age.

Again, Bill, I had no memory of this letter of yours on the Autumn Equinox of 1985, which is echoing mine today on the Spring Equinox of 2023. Although, pausing a moment... actually I *do* have a sliver of memory about the name **Kenelm Digby** because of you saying it might be connected with DF through the mutual motto.

On the other hand your mention of Sherborne did give me a small frisson. I've been muttering to Margaret for weeks that we should go there, a day trip, even though I know nothing about the place other than that it looked pretty in the photos I'd seen. So... have you been nudging me to go there the past few weeks, or is it my own Self prodding you? Or has everyone else who might be reading this exchange of letters between us been contributing also? Everything that *can* happen *does* happen, as the quantumists say.

There's a button on the side of my big, clumsy Tesco smart phone. Now that the people have gone I press and ask: *How far is it from here to Sherborne?*

A woman's voice replies: *32 miles.*

It must be like the Direct Voice communication that Victorian spiritualists would get via their floating 'trumpets'. I think you would have loved such a phone yourself, given that your favourite god was Hermes and you were in The Signals during the War, and thus loved the arts of Communication on every level. 32 miles and 32 Paths on the Tree of the Life you once planted in many peoples' psyches.

So, I must make Sherborne happen soon.

Kenelm Digby... No, I didn't take you up on your suggestion to look him up. In those pre-internet days it would have meant a drive in my rickety but beloved Citroen 2V to the very small library at Bradford on Avon with little chance of finding much about him there. I certainly didn't have the wherewithal to track back from the Firth Dynasty that began in 19th Century Yorkshire, to see if it connected with Digby in the 17th Century. But as you say, they may have been connected, and you might find some justification about the 'Bloodmother' behind everything? I'll leave that sort of thing to any young whipper-snappers with more time and money than sense, and I'll try to find that book of yours via Google again.

I have to say that for me, Word Processors and the Internet are among the most wonderful things in my lifetime. I do think that the latter is, somehow, a manifestation of what some still call the Akashic Records. Everything, they insist, can be found in the Halls of Akasha if you know how and where to look. But, as I learned from that delightful phoney Lobsang Rampa, you only access the historical events through the eyes of the participants whose minds your enter, and everyone sees/experiences/understands/interprets things differently. There is no such thing as objective Truth; there is no such person as a single Bill Gray.

But *Kenelm Digby, Kenelm Digby...* it's such a powerful name isn't it? I've sometimes regretted not adopting a pen-name at the beginning of my writing career. I've never liked 'Alan Richardson'. It's a stupid, un-rhythmic name. But 'William G. Gray' has a certain ring, doesn't it? Better than 'Gordon Gray' as your Mum called you.

Kenelm Digby... let me send a signal 'out there' (which is also 'in here') and see if he/it responds.

Years ago I tried this with Abaris, whom John Wood the Elder believed was *the* great Magician of the West. And also the one-time Grand Master of the Templars with the splendid name of Amberaldus, about whom nothing is known by anyone, even though he was certainly an historical figure.

Did either of them respond and 'come through' to me like one of DF's 'Chiefs', bringing me channelled messages?

Erm... no, not in the obvious sense. But I did seem to have flows of events, energies, synchronisations that were constant in my life during the writing of *Searching for Sulis*, that must have come via Abaris. Likewise for *The Templar Door* with respect to Amberaldus.

Perhaps the latter was the Templar knight that a psychic saw standing quietly and patiently next to me when I was chatting to Paddy Slade at

North Stoke? Or perhaps Amberaldus was a 'past life' in the usual understanding of that concept, as yet unremembered by me. Or was it an aspect of you!?

As dear *dear* Arthur Guirdham once wrote with respect to this sort of thing, *We are One Another.*

Aren't we?

And while I think on, if you were struck by Sherborne Abbey with its Benedictine background, the most extraordinary place *I've* ever known was the Templar church of St Michael at Garway, in the lush, still-hidden borderlands between England and Wales, that Jacques de Molay made a special trip to visit in the last few peaceful weeks before he went back to France where he was arrested, tortured and forced to recant.

I've never known energies/atmospheres to compare with what we experienced when we did our own simple internal magick at Garway.

That was, *is!* a true Holy Place, and probably was millennia before Christianity was invented…

Alan

Wm. G. Gray
14. Bennington St.
Cheltenham
Glos. GL50 4ED

Telephone

(0242) 24129

12 OCT 1985

Dear Alan

Subsequent to our telephone conversation I located the "Loveday" grave picture in a most unlikely pile. As you see it doesn't give much information except the date of death, and if you notice that is the same as with Dion Fortune's grave too. No birthdate. Deathdate only. Co-incidence? To the best of my knowledge the name is purely coincidental with Raoul's who I believe turned into a Buddhist monk after quitting Crowley.

 I was sorry to hear of CH's death, but at over 90 one is entitled to die and get the hell out of this miserable world. God preserve me from living to such a dreadful extension.

 Oh yes I remember Mary Gilchrist quite well and liked her a lot. Her cousin "Robbie" was a dear old chap and remarkably psychic. I remember the first time we met, after a while he suddenly reached forward and touched me on the throat saying; "You needn't worry about that it'll soon clear." He had touched the one spot I was worried about at the time, and I hadn't said a word to give any clues whatsoever, nor did Mary know anything about it either.

 Mary had been a professional medium but gave it up entirely on DF's insistence. She was a Yorkshire woman with a keen and typical sense of humour and "downrightness". Robbie was a retired dental surgeon who explained to me the technicalities of how infected teeth poisoned the whole system and were undoubtedly the cause of my arthritis. They were both quite elderly people when I knew them. DF had left her the Chalice Orchard property which she later sold to Geoffrey Ashe.

 I imagine that since she had given up a livelihood at DF's dictates, DF felt she owed Mary _something_ in return. I doubt if Mary had much to live on beyond the OAP and Robbie's tiny pension. Robbie died rather quietly, and I remember how Mary said she kept seeing a gold light around the coffin which seemed to fade out during the funeral service. She went to live with some other relative afterwards and we never saw her again.

I don't remember much about the "Carstairs" contact. There were odd mentions of it in the IL papers, none of which I still have by the way, because they were terribly stuffy, boring, and unappealing in the extreme, mostly consisting of strictures and moralising without any particular "human" or sympathetic touch whatever. They just didn't <u>reach</u> a sentient soul at all, being aimed entirely at abstruse intellectual levels of appreciation. My guess is that "Carstairs" could have been an alter-ego she invented for the Animus part of herself, though I don't see any reason why it should not have been a genuine contact. You have to remember the millions of young and very active minds that were suddenly killed during the Great War, most of them with their last thought being something like: "My God I've got to make people see the stupidity of this", coupled to the burning intention of at least <u>trying</u> to get that message through somehow into the minds and souls of those still alive.

I know damn well that none of those I knew during the last War had any thoughts about how nice and noble it would be to die for "democracy", when we all knew we would only die for profiteers' pockets and politicians' promises. We had seen our fathers' generation conned into that sort of grave, and all we hoped for was to avoid the same fate. To this day I can't view any young child without a terrible sense of pity mixed with hope for its future, plus a prayer that I'll be allowed to die before the whole horror starts up again, because the hell we went through will look like a Sunday School treat compared to what they will face. God help them.

Curious thing is that as you see Loveday died <u>after</u> DF, so who arranged the grave-space???? I haven't a clue. Anyway good wishes and
KQ.

Bill

The Garden Office   23/24 March 2023

Hello Bill – and Bobbie!

Carstairs…He *was* a Mystery wasn't he? Of all the messages from the Inner Plane Adeptii that have been channelled within the IL, it was only his that sounded real. He/It communicated in a style and tone entirely in keeping with his human persona as a soldier killed during the Great War, and something of a cheery, cheeky chappy. If you'd ever seen Gareth Knight's excellent biography of DF (written with full and enviable access to the FIL archives), you'd see Carstairs even had a light-hearted dig at me within the Lodge after my book *Priestess* came out! *I want Flanders not slanders!* he exclaimed through the mediator. That made me chuckle. 'Carstairs,' as I've often whispered into the aethyrs,'you can come through to me any time.' Though he never has. Well, not in any ways that I can yet understand.

Chain of associations here now Bill…

Remember your witchpal Doreen Valiente? And Gerald Gardner's claim to have been initiated in Witchcraft by a certain 'Dorothy Cluttterbuck'? Everyone mocked the very idea of the latter, but Doreen apparently proved, after laborious research, that she Clutterbuck exist. I hope that one day some young Googler will prove that Carstairs also did exist. And so for anyone is reading this, here is the only clue I have… Alan Adams told me that 'David Carstairs' was his *birth* name; his mother remarried when he was young, and it was under his step-father's still-unknown surname that he enlisted and was soon killed.

Loveday… I was wrong about him being Raoul. He was Charles Thomas Loveday, Magical Name *Amor Vincit Omnia.* I think that's on his gravestone. His wife of many years was devastated when AVO abandoned her for this Miss Firth. He in turn must have been equally gutted when Merl arrived and Miss Firth became Mrs Evans. At least the old guy got a grave near DF's and so got to sleep with his beloved 'Rhea' forever. He was a fool for love, perhaps. We've all been Lovedays in our time, haven't we?

I had a restless night last night, during heavy rain storm. I had to go into the spare room so as not to wake M. and scribbled notes before I forgot.

Perhaps like those that you described Marcia keeping. Somehow, I kept thinking about this name or concept of Abaris.

I feel that Carstairs, if he really had no historical existence, was an exemplar of the Unknown Soldier, who sacrificed himself (or was sacrificed) for King and Country under the sacred and almost forgotten notion that the Land and the People are One.

Perhaps 'Abaris the Hyperborean' was/is an exemplar of the Western Mysteries and the Tradition you have helped work through here in Britain. So the Names and Identities were constructs that helped connect with Energies that can be felt as Entities. Or is it vice-versa? Like the powerful sonic 'Dad!' that has an infinite variety of utterances that have proved capable of invoking all sorts of responses at every level.

That's a damned clever idea if you ask me, Bill! But I expect you knew that already.

Abaris Abaris Abaris...travelling the world with an arrow.

We'll see how that works out, if at all.

I don't remember asking about Mary Gilchrist at all. This is definitely an Age Thing, though *your* Thing seems to be in better nick than mine at the moment. If I'd met her and 'Robbie' I'd have glued them into my brain cells because I'm more attracted to 'remarkably psychic' people than the average Adeptii, who often aren't very psychic at all and just bring through tosh from Inner Planes that has no value for me personally. Present day professional mediums like Melanie Kellaway from Weston super Mare and Joanie Goddard from Trowbridge have brought through messages from my hopeless, unlearned, irritating, deeply-missed and adored-too-late ex-coal miner Dad - messages that have been transformative in a way that puts stuff like Angelic or Inner Plane Adept communications in the shade.

In fact I've been trying for some time to seek out or just stumble upon someone like 'Robbie'. Apart from my heart and bladder I've lifelong problems with my Eustachian tubes. I want someone hands-on, but those I've approached keep telling me it's to do with me 'not listening' on spiritual levels; and so they try to do Quantum Healing on me involving semi-hypnotic regression and past lives. I've been soft enough to let them, but nothing has worked.

Hmmm... our blackbird that we call Meatloaf, who has made several appearances in some of my books has just appeared and is nagging me for his mealworms. One moment...

Now, sorry about that Bill; I know you won't mind hanging on because you're in a Timeless realm. Or is it me?

So... Robbie... some of it's coming back to me now. Maybe the blackbird nudged me. Didn't they call him '*Uncle* Robbie'? Someone who was doing psychic research into the Work of Seymour and Hartley after reading one of my books, wove a certain 'Robert Firth' into his narrative, stating it to be Dion Fortune's *actual* uncle. It made a helluva story and 'Uncle Robert Firth' played a good part in the derring-do. I think Satanists were involved. They were probably hooded. Why are the baddies always hooded? But there was no such person on this plane or any inner plane. It was a good book though, but a bit daft. I won't mention the psychic's name, because other stuff he has done has been brilliant and bewildering and I've bought every one of them. Of course I'm jealous.

And the Memory Thing has just made something else spring forward and start tapping like the blackbird....

Perhaps the last time I saw Christine Hartley was in her retirement flat at Hyde Gate in Winchester (a hint of the Parallel Life I could/should/might have had?) and she mentioned the detective novels that Dion Fortune wrote under a pseudonym. The very few in the IL who knew about these had obviously kept very quiet, but Christine had been DF's agent.

What? What?!!! I cried.

Christine couldn't remember. Such information is pure gold for any biographer. If I'd known how to a Vulcan Mind Meld with her I would have done so then, though you'll have to look inside my mind now, Bill, to see what *that* might be.

It was only as I was about to leave, at the very last moment as I stood on the threshold of her front door (damned magical places, thresholds!), that she burst out... 'Steele. V.M. Steele. She wrote detective novels under that name.'

These were all in a totally different style to those shed wrote as 'Dion Fortune'. And filled with the racial stereotypes of her era that would make people bristle today, though – alas – not trouble you at all.

Best,

Alan

Wm. G. Gray
14. Bennington St.
Cheltenham
Glos. GL50 4ED

Telephone

(0242) 24129

Dear Alan, [Undated]
Thanks for your prompt reply, and sorry to hear you've got the bugs.

Yes, "L" was indeed the first letter of my then magical name which was quite a complicated one.

I have really no idea why Jacobus just refuses to answer my letters. Marcia writes regularly, even scrappy notes, and of course I'm sending off a couple of pages of script to her every week as notes for this book on earthing we're doing together, which she's getting on with. I'm just doing notes, suggestions, and little tales, while she's bulking them out and shaping them up. Making a god job of it from what I can see.

Of course Weisers are throwing out my stuff now that old Carr's dollars aren't behind me any more, and Llewellyns are taking it all up. This "Goddess" " book was originally the Bloodmother, which Jacobus wanted to do for about 5 years and did bugger all with it, so I hastily rewrote the lot and shoved it off to Llewellyn, then after they accepted it, I had a brilliant flash as to what the <u>Christian</u> Holy Grail actually was <u>in fact</u>, wrote it up and sent it along, so they duly included it, and there we were.

Some Anglican cleric has obligingly compiled all the ancient consecration formulae, and there we were again - it was all too obvious. So far as I know I am the first and so far only writer to specify exactly what the genuine Holy Grail (Christian version) was. So the "Quest" was in no sense a fiction but a reality which has not yet been achieved, because that would mean writing in an acknowledgement of the Feminine Holy Spirit's involvement with the Motherhood of Jesus in the consecration formula in the Liturgy. One sees quite clearly now why the Cathars would only accept St Johns Gospel. And a lot of other things appear plain that were hitherto obscure. OK, the Grail Cultists may not have achieved the Quest they wanted, but they did the next best thing and got the Virgin Mary promoted to virtually Goddess status with a hell of a lot of jiggery pokery and finagling around. I'm surprised in a way that nobody's written to denounce me as 'being utterly wrong and totally inaccurate.

Tom Lawless of Llewellyns who processes my books, makes an incredibly good job of them. Only about three unimportant errors, (typos and such) in the whole of the proofs and with Weisers there were usually 50-60 or so, I did complain about the "flashy" and what I thought cheap and nasty covers, but this last one was my own design in fact.

Next one they're bringing out is "Self Made by Magic" under another name, and then they'll do the old "Rollright Ritual" (again under another title, Weiser wouldn't even touch it), but its the sort of pseudo "Witch" thing which Llewellyns like to handle.

Anyway, Jacobus has got enough to worry about with this craziness of Du Klerks. You just don't know what'll happen to South Africa… It wouldn't surprise me if they had Civil War. You can't possibly know nor would you probably believe what's going on. However it would be a waste of time even trying to tell you, so I won't.

But thanks for listening, I shouldn't think you'll ever get the truth out of Jacobus, but you could go through all his letters if you cared to bother. There's a huge heap here, and a lot of tapes too.

Where did you get that bit bf info about Crowley watching the same Zeppelin burning? I was only 4-5 at the time. Poor old Crowley, I've known of other mothers who walked in on their screwing sons and all they said was: "Er - would you like a cup of tea?" Fact. What the hell would Crowley be doing at Ramsgate in about 1917 anyway? '

    Good wishes,

Bill

Cafe #1   25th March 2023

Bill…

Magical Names… Of course I've crafted several for myself over the years, starting with 'Mahananda', before I knew about the Western Mystery Tradition, then through to 'Ariston Metron' during my miserable year in Gloucester, plus a number since that aren't worth mentioning. If yours at the last is 'L' then mine is 'T', and neither of us will ever reveal. Although that said, I'm not good at keeping secrets of any kind for anyone.

Marcia Pickands and Jacobus Schwartz… I liked the former very much; I never 'empathed' with the latter, as you would have put it. Then again I never 'empathed' with Marion Green after her horrible review of my *Gate of Moon*. Yet I have to admit that she, like yourself, has done tremendous and unceasing Work for the Western Mysteries over the decades since. She was older than me but I think she's still alive. Perhaps if she hadn't given me that rotten review we'd have become BFF's as the youngsters of today put it.

I've never claimed to be a grown-up.

I think I was wrong about the Zeppelin.

But Bill, Bill, Bill… I haven't the slightest understanding of your comments about the 'genuine Holy Grail (Christian version)'. Also, forgive me, but I don't want or *need* to understand them – any more than you will appreciate my arguments that GlasVegasbury, as I call it, is an increasingly tawdry phoney like some of the folk who pour there with localised equivalents of Jerusalem Syndrome. (Do I see flames coming out of your nostrils?)

What is Jerusalem Syndrome? - I'm making you ask. It's recognised as an acute psychotic state involving the presence of religiously themed obsessive ideas, delusions, or other psychosis-like experiences that are triggered by a visit there. Plus *historically* the town cannot possibly have had *anything* to do with 'Avalon'! Remember me mentioning that fella who channeled 'Robert Firth'? Well, among many other genuine researchers, he demonstrated this quite clearly in a superbly written book in which he legitimately 'channeled' proper historians.

I think the nonsense around the town is down to a certain Dr Goodchild and that woman who wrote 'Avalon of the Heart' – you know who. Last year before my heart attack I gave a guided tour of the Limpley Stoke Valley to a woman who was convinced that in a previous life *she* had written that book, being Dion Fortune reborn.

I made no judgement as ever, other than to point out (nicely I hope) that she was not the first I'd met believing that.

Perhaps we are ALL Dion Fortune reborn…

            All the best

alan

Wm. G. Gray
14. Bennington St.
Cheltenham
Glos. GL50 4ED

Telephone

(0242) 24129

31ˢᵗ March 1987

Dear Alan,
Back from South Africa I've just read your latest book "Priestess", and must congratulate you on a remarkable piece of research which should clear up a lot of puzzlement amongst those who value Fortune's work, though it seemed to me there was something missing, and for the life of me I can't quite put a finger on it. Like my BloodMother book which my friend in South Africa will publish this year with any luck.

Weisers will reprint "Ladder of Lights" some time this summer, and next year my "A Self made by Magic" should be reprinted in South Africa. My Sangreal Tarot ought to be out by this autumn.

The Temple out there is doing very well, and in May this year I am supposed to be visiting the USA (New York State) to see what they have done out there for the Sodality. Only for a fortnight IF Bobbie's health permits. She is having a lot of trouble with mouth ulcers, and needs hospital treatment to clear it up. They think it will be OK for me to go then, but who can be certain?

I'm still doing a bit of Chiropody, but I will have to retire this year. At 74 it's a bit much for arthritic hands which are losing their steadiness. I would almost say it's ridiculous.

You know I'm going to say an odd thing that maybe you can understand. My impression is that you gave a much better impression of the real Dion Fortune with your one chapter in "Dancers to the Gods" than you did with the whole of "Priestess". I don't say you did badly at all, but somehow you made her live with the single chapter 'Priestess in the Orchard', whereas with "Priestess" you were discussing the antecedents of a dead woman and all her peculiarities. I can't explain better than that I'm afraid. Anyway it's a damn sight better than the one Carr Collins paid for and I congratulate you.

Jacobus has my autobiography draft, and he will probably tackle it after my death. As you know, DF had a horror of anyone trying to drag back her past personality as it was instead of trying to contact the still existent soul she hoped to become. I can agree with her there. She wasn't a perfect person and knew that very well as I do myself. Some medium said a while back: "DF seems to have become a lot mellower since she died." Which meant that she appeared to be a lot more tolerant and understanding of human weaknesses. When living, she was inclined to be very critical of human behaviour and made this quite plain to those concerned. Her standards were apt to be over-rigid, but she never expected anyone to do what she could not do herself, or would not have attempted if she felt it to be a proper course of conduct.

I wasn't very close to her myself and we disagreed on a number of points, but one thing we had in common. We were as faithful to our Tradition as we could be and served it as we believed best because we felt it <u>was</u> the best - for our particular breed.

Let that be our epitaph. 'We sought to serve'. Whether we did in fact or not is for others to judge, but at least we can honestly say we tried.

Anyway, God Bless you and the family KQ,

I think there is a lot left for you to bring out yet.

Bill

The Atrium   31st March 2023

Hello Bill,
Today we're **exactly** 36 years apart!

Thanks for your kind words about *Priestess*. I can dine out on comments like that for months. I did the best I could with the limited resources I had then, under very difficult circumstances, and I've been moan-boasting about about this ever since. Or is the word 'humble-bragging'? I probably did both. Later, 'Thoth Publications' brought out a second edition - with a contract that (I didn't realise) never included dates of any royalty payments. When I twigged, I had to fight for the pitiful sums accrued. However, by the time of doing this much-needed second edition I had a word processor and was able to access the World Wide Web, correct the early mistakes and look at DF in greater depth. Particularly with respect to the Spirit of Place that had/has come to obsess me, centred around Limpley Stoke where her parents met, courted and married.

New York State... that would be Marcia Pickands. Her martial arts name was White Crane, and she spent some time teaching the CIA how to kill with their bare hands. My kind of woman! NYS is where you're going to be reborn, Bill, if there *is* such a process, or if it's not the wishful thinking of a young American mum (not Marcia!). The 'next you' must be about 20 now and has made no attempt to track me down.

Yes, I did eventually meet Marcia and liked her a lot. Years after her death in 2016 the at tender age of 62, her husband Marty came over to spend time with his son, who was a Major in the US Army briefly seconded to the big British Army base in nearby Warminster. He gave me lots of your letters to Marcia, so I've got a *Third* Tranche here now, though I won't do anything with this lot. They are brilliant and provocative as you guided her step-by-step into the very heart of the Sangreal Mysteries. If anyone else reading this now should want to 'do' something with these, then they can suck up to me in due course and prove their worth. Though I've no doubt they'll end up being sold on E-Bay when my back is turned.

I notice that in *this* lot of letters, you never once mention Marion Green, but you spend a lot of time complaining about Jacobus, even getting a magically-potent Italian woman to launch a Current of Reproach against him. I've heard that Italians make the best assassins.

'We sought to Serve' you write. Of course the Oath suggested by DF was 'I Desire to Know in order to Serve'. I do believe that. Sometimes I've inverted it to say: 'I Desire to Serve in order to Know', and that has sometimes been more appropriate. Although I can hear your own sharp response, echoing the thought you had during your initiation into the SIL: 'Serve *What*, Serve *Who*?'

Come to think of it, I have no clear answer to that riposte of yours. Perhaps, if I'm being a bit pompous (I can be very pompous), it might be: 'I Desire to Serve *Magick* in order to Know.' But doesn't that sound twattish!

Last night I watched for about the third time *Indiana Jones and the Crystal Skull*. Bobbie would have loved it because I know she was (like the young me) deeply into Science Fiction, and was close to the writer Michael Moorcock. You'd have enjoyed it too but would probably have kept up a running commentary on how they got *everything* wrong. But there is my favourite scene in which Cate Blanchett stands before the long-headed crystalline, inter-dimensional Being who has been hiding in the 'space between spaces' and asks, for her reward in serving them: *I want to know I want to **Know**...*

I'd probably ask exactly the same, even if my head did explode because of it.

Oh and there is one fragmented piece by you that I really enjoyed, in which you describe similar inter-dimensional Beings at the beginning of Humanity. I'll cut and paste now because it's imporant, and I might lose it again in the 'space between the spaces' as they said in the film…

What puzzles me is why you should be so concerned with the identity of our so-called "Guides"… A long time ago they used to be called the "Watchers" because that's all they did. Watched Humanity to see how we were developing, but didn't actually do anything one way or the other. Neither helped nor harmed. They might pass an opinion or possibly offer some advice IF they took all that much interest in you (which was seldom), but because they had a clear perception of what was going on in this world and the most likely outcome of what would result. It was advantageous to try and persuade them to communicate –

if they would. They were usually quite indifferent to the casual fate of humans, much as we might be about insects or even microbes, but <u>sometimes</u> they <u>might</u> be maneuvered into extending a "hand" in our direction if we showed signs of any particular ability or interest. Names? Don't mean a thing to them as identity. Qualities have more significance. In other words they aren't sweet and loving critters any more than laboratory technicians are "caring" specialists for their bench animals. They are here to see that a particular process takes place, and that is that. Keep relationships with them "right" and things do well, but get them wrong and they'll come unstuck...Neither Marcia nor I have any illusions about the nature of the so-called "Spirit Guides" we are dealing with.

There are a lot of books out now by leading researchers that talk at length about these Watchers, digging up all sorts of material from arcane sources. But *your* info seems to come from actual memory of them! That's what I like. That's what make you a *real* magician.

                Bestest

                Alan

Wm. G. Gray
14. Bennington St.
Cheltenham
Glos. GL50 4ED

Telephone

(0242) 24129

10 SEPT 1987

Dear Alan,

A few quick words of thanks. I haven't a clue when or even IF Jacobus will ever send back my autobiography, what's happened to him, or anything else, but I'll certainly mention it to him WHEN I write which could be quite a while yet since he has to write me first.

I'm amazed to hear your books don't seem to be selling all that well, BUT are you sure Aquarian aren't twisting you??? As I told you they twisted me something rotten. Llewellyns don't pay at all that I know of, and it was only to place the work somewhere and get rid of it that I let them have it. Had I been younger I'd never have let it go. But at my age who cares???? But, if a biography of Dion Fortune doesn't sell all that well, what chance would there be for one concerning Bill Gray, a relatively undistinguished nonentity of supreme unimportance???? But thanks a lot for the offer. If you ever do get the autobiography, KEEP ANY CASH you might get for it. Bobbie and I will both be dead, and I haven't anyone to leave anything to. No family. I thought of making Jacobus my literary executor, but God knows if that's any use.

I was pleased to hear though that my "Magical Ritual Methods" will be reissued. There still isn't anything like it around, for reasons I've never understood. Actually I wrote "MRM" because when I was first concerned with ritual work there was no such thing available. You were supposed to learn from watching others and doing what they did, but nobody ever told you the whys and wherefores - or ever made them clear if they tried. For instance nobody ever told me that a red Sanctuary lamp went right back to primitive times when fire as a sacred element had to be guarded on a ledge in a cave where it would not be extinguished by flash floods sweeping through the cavern. It marked the "God place" because it <u>was</u> the God on whom the whole of human civilisation depended. So it had to be tended by nine maidens who later became Vestals, and subsequently ordinary nuns. It was the one Spark from which all other fires could be rekindled if they went out, but without Fire, what would any human community be???? Exactly. Powerless.

Also in Christian Churches the red Lamp could be seen best through thick smoke and it marked the place where the sacred vessels were kept, so if the place were on fire, rescuers could see where to try and rescue the sacred things from. It also stood for the Precious Blood, which meant Salvation. etc. But was this ever explained as clearly as that? No. All that took me years to find out bit by bit.

There is still an enormous amount of research to be done in parallel directions for anyone interested. Why nine Maidens? Three actually tending the fire, three chasing up fresh fuel, and three off duty turn and turn around, Besides the nine months of pregnancy behind a human birth. Incidentally, so far as I know the Parsee fire-worshippers are supposed to be the oldest organised religion on earth that can trace their origins back to the Stone Age, though how they can do this I'm damned if I know. Still, it was our control of Fire which put us ahead of all other species on earth. And what have we done with it? God help us we have replaced all the prehistoric natural monsters with a Fire so MONSTROUS, it makes them look like midgets of insignificance. Think of that when you next light a candle.

What am I working on you ask? Surprisingly - Satanism, but from a very odd angle, which I'm tentatively titling "Sensible Satanism". If Satan was once part of God and will be once more at the END OF THINGS and assuming he is now the Archetypal Arch-enemy of humanity, since we were told to love our enemies and do good to they that persecute us, who should we love most? According to Jesus - Satan, whom legend has it was his twin brother. It is not exactly a "Save our Satan" campaign, but a different outlook on the Devil. It may not be a popular idea for selling. Readers want the slurp and the slap, the twiddles and fiddles, and all the dirty little details of who stuck what into whom and where, and most importantly how. but there isn't any of that. There's a little legend in the Mishna I think, that every time Man sins, Satan sheds a single tear because that will prolong his exile from Heaven just that much more, Further that Satan himself IS the Lapis exilis from which the miraculous Holy Grail was supposed to be fashioned.

So in a vague way, my book is a sort of "Save our Satan" thing, not exactly a rehabilitation, or a defence, or a "Wet Liberal" thing so much as a utilitarian one, pointing out that "Satan" and "God" are simply opposite ends of the same ENERGY, and you can't have one without the other any more than you can have such a thing as a one-ended stick, or a single pole magnet, If you like to look at it in a vulgar light, Satan is God's arsehole, BUT we <u>need</u> arseholes, and without them we wouldn't live very long.

So yes, Satan does exist. He is the personification of all the Evil in humanity and God knows that's terrifying enough. Definitely real. I wish. it wasn't, but you mustn't forget it is ENERGY. And as Energy it can be done something with.

It's finished, but will take me weeks yet to typescript. Half ready already, but another hundred pp to go yet.

More enquiries from the USA about starting a Sangreal Sodality Group in the Bronx, of all horrible districts. Still I'll let Marcia cope with that one.

God Bless and KQ.

Bill

The Atrium   late March 2023

Hello Bill

I haven't a clue what date it is! That's one good thing about being long-retired: days and dates and flow seamlessly into each other faster than the speed of light. The U3A are gathering here again for their weekly walking group. Mind you there's an air of trepidation about them because the rain is *hammering* down on the high glass roof, probably making it seem fiercer outside than it actually is. However, 'neither hail nor rain nor dark of night...' etc. will stop them. Putin is currently threatening the world with nuclear destruction but the U3A is marching boldly onward. Who said the British were no longer plucky! (Personally I've never plucked in my life, and must put that on my bucket list.)

Sensible Satanism is a brilliant title, decades ahead of its time. I suppose I should Google what happened to it but I'm a bit weary today. Maybe I'm picking your own angst over Bobbie's understandable fears. I don't want to get distracted and end up down a rabbit-hole as has happened to me too often in the past. Rabbit-holes, as I understand them, are dead-ends in damp darkness. Perhaps I should modernise and hope for a worm-hole instead, and that would whizz me through Space and Time to other galaxies.

Satan… I'll give Him/It a miss. I do know about Darkness though, no-one better than me. Honest. My slim book *Dark Magery* was all about Darkness, though you'd probably have picked it apart as being trivial in comparison with yours on Satanism. You'd probably have corrected every statement. I do know that Darkness is not synonymous with Evil, any more than Light is always about Goodness.

And – you won't remember – it was actually *you* who triggered my own ideas. In one of my early visits to you in late 1973, just as I was leaving to catch the last bus back to Gloucester, you asked me:

What bears light?

Eh? was my immortal reply. I remember that you snorted.

*Duh...If you think of Light as being an **energy**, what bears it?*

Erm… a torch?

No! (you didn't actually *Stupid boy!* but it was implied) *If you think of energies, then Light is born by **Darkness**.*

Of course today, with the kind of synchronicity that would have meant something to you, I've had my yearly email from 'Immanion Press' detailing this year's sales of my brilliant novel *The Lightbearer*. This is based upon a fragment of a past/other/alternative/parallel life involving a young American paratroop dropped into France in 1944. It should have been made into a film, but all those possibilities faded like Faery Gold and it lay dormant for many years until the late Storm Constantine took it on.

As it's only 7 pence, they'll hang onto it and the similar royalties for the previous years since it was published until it all comes to over £10.00.

Of course I'd like 'proper' royalties for this and other books I've done. But as you said yourself, using all the power of your four question marks: '*...at my age who cares????*'

Your bit about Satan/Arsehole is a good 'un. I've no longer got any interest in the Kabbalah (and I've got Murry Hope to thank for that as well) but I do remember in your brilliant *Ladder of Lights* describing Daath as effectively the cosmic arsehole, a Sephirah that was of particular interest to Kenneth Grant, whom you felt was a wrong 'un. (As did Basil Wilby.) In your scheme, Malkuth was once in the place of Daath on the Cosmic Tree and then it sort of 'Fell'. So the way I saw it, then Daath (Knowledge) and Malkuth (Experience) have this curious connection. Actually that's not the right word, but you can work around it. So I was very struck by a quote from Osman Spare that went: 'Knowledge is the excrement of Experience'. Forgetting about the kabbalibosh for a moment, I do think that is true.

I've got the original MS of your autobiography in a box in our bedroom. Can't remember who sent it. Perhaps yourself?

Alan

Wm. G. Gray
14. Bennington St.
Cheltenham
Glos. GL50 4ED

Telephone

(0242) 24129

Dear Alan,

Just recently I've had an enquiry from London from some people who are interested in starting up a Sangreal Group in the UK, and I should be seeing at least some of than fairly soon, They sounded quite nice people on the phone and by letter. Oddly enough, this bod is a Kung Fu Instructor also, but works for the LCC on some "Youth Training" program. His young woman associate seems to be a secretary of some sort. Anyway they've rung up and I've fixed to go and meet them. So we'll see what'll happen at that point. I've no great hopes myself, but if the Sangreal is anything at all it should be able to manage what it wants for itself, and if it can't then – bugger it.

    I'd really like to get that going before I finally pop off and then you can get on with that biog which I still feel is a waste of your time and energy. But as regards cash, well please do feel quite free to pocket anything whatever you can get IF you ever get anything which I really doubt. Point is I don't have anyone in the world to leave anything to. No relatives and few enough friends.

    I'm sure you'll be sorry to hear of Bobbie's trouble. Malignancy in the mouth. Oh she's had the full RT treatment and responded OK, but attends every so often for checks. Smoking caused it of course. Fortunately we have about the latest Cobalt unit here which is producing remarkable results. We've just had her brother from New Zealand over here on a bit of holiday stayed with us a fortnight. He has no interest in the occult in the least, so we didn't have much to talk about, but otherwise he's quite a nice chap. Could be the double of old Sid James the actor.

    I must now push on with more letters, a scad of stuff in the mail for me today. One from Jacobus, who seems to be in the shit financially owing to trusting the wrong person. But otherwise apart from his chronic bad health – OK. He is still messing about with my

Bloodmother book, but it doesn't look as if he'll ever do much with it except balls it up.

God Bless and KQ

Bill

Fairfield Opportunity Farm Café   31st March?? 2023

Dear Bill,

Scribbling here while M. is at the hairdresser. It's a cheery old-fashioned tea-room in Dilton Marsh run by adults with Learning Disabilities. Apart from my last ten years running a specialist Mobile Library, for the elderly, across remote parts of Wiltshire, I've spent most of my working life with this category of people. Some of them, I am sure, are faery beings having a go at being 'human' for the first time and often struggling. Mind you, even humans struggle at being human, so you can't look down on the Folk for that. However one professional psychic we know is convinced that many of them are somewhat malign souls of extra-terrestrial origin, and she's rather afraid of them. I don't go along with that, although the psychic in question is exceptional.

I wonder what your 'Bloodmother' – Whoever or Whatever she is – would make of these people? Inferior? Failed experiments? Listen Bill, many of the ones I've worked with have more Grace than you or I will ever know. One of the most important 'teachers' and largest souls I've ever met was the late Carlo Torczuk. Polish-Italian. Couldn't read or write or count. Had speech and hearing impediments on top of his Down's Syndrome. Was overweight, often irresponsible, and obsessed with the film *Star Wars*. But he treated *every* woman he met, no matter how old, young, fat, skinny, cross-eyed, batty, loud-mouthed and mad – he treated each one as if they were most beautiful and interesting woman in the world. Of course they adored him. He was a Babe Magnet decades before the term was invented.

Would the Bloodmother have approved of him? What the hell is She/It? Or should I now say 'They'? I really must find out what you mean, if only because I had an upbringing marred and scarred by a very human 'Dark Mother', as described in my book *Geordie's War*. I should contact Jacobus, but as I never empathed years ago, and I can't say that age will have mellowed my feelings.

For myself, I didn't go into this line of work because of any goodness on my part, but simply because I couldn't get a 'proper' job at the time. Even though the pay was crap, the hours long, the aggressions (of some clients) were extreme, this category of people taught me more than any other. So... if my own Self did somehow choose my present life, would I do this sort of work again - perhaps in that parallel quantum realm involving the Winchester time-line?

No.

There's a good wi-fi signal in this cafe. Better than in the Atrium, actually. Apparently the Earth is about to be hit by a gigantic flare from our dodgy-looking Sun, but I'm sitting happily here amid the grey-haired knitting ladies and their village gossip and googling what happened to your Sangreal Sodality, *Sensible Satanism* and particularly your *Bloodmother.* Maybe I've haven't searched deep enough but the only reference to the Sodality is in Philadelphia, and they suggest sending a hand-written letter with photograph in order to make contact. That sounds pretty feeble to me.

But Bobbie, dear Bobbie... I did like her, very much. I have to say something about her. Because you were such a powerful figure, Bill, I know many people assumed that she must have been a put-upon housewife, knowing her place, attending to your every whim. As she would have replied: *Balls to that!*

I remember that she had her own, soft power. When I last visited you in 1974, I'd just had the Longest Day in Hell, caused by my teaching job in Gloucester, where I made every mistake I should NEVER have made with the very pupils best able to rip me apart. I was a wreck when I turned up and you were less than impressed. After all, you had been machine-gunned and bombed at Dunkirk. That pretty much trumped what I'd been getting from the little fuckers in class 4K. Yet while I shrank deeper into my misery and you and Norman Gibb(?) ignored me, Bobbie gave me tea and warmth and simple chat.

Ach... enough of that! To be honest, if the situation had been reversed, I don't suppose I would have acted *any* differently. I'm not much good with the *There there theres...* of life.

(Somehow, I've got the MS of Bobbie's unpublished novel with its alternative titles, including: *Bloody Instructions; Poisoned Chalice; The Barronswood Devil.* Did you give me this? I've no idea as to the worth of her writing, as I rarely read fiction. I think, Bill, that you should act as an Inner Plane Agent and get it sorted. Or are you too busy being incarnate in America now, or else existing in the Perfect Peace Profound that you felt was the Ultimate?)

That was the night you didn't walk me back to the bus station as you usually did. You didn't give me that strange handshake with the two fingers on my wrist that might have been a Masonic thing. Isn't that the grip of a Master Mason? Were you 'On the Level' as I think they say? Instead you gave me an almost ritualistic *Goodbye* on the very narrow and liminal place of your doorstep in Bennington Street, making it quite clear that our relationship was over. I was effectively Banished. That was in this time of year in early 1974, near exactly 49 years ago.

You know Bill, if we ever met today you'd put me in the same class as Bobbie's brother, no more than a 'nice chap' with not much conversation about 'the things that matter'. But you saying that, now that I'm no longer afraid, here's something that has always bothered me…

I could enter any group today with a notional intent to discuss 'occult' topics and mention, for example, that I was deeply into the G.D. or the O.T.O. or the T.S. and a dozen other well-known esoteric acronyms. But if I were to pipe up and express an interest in the **S.S**. then eyebrows would raise and people would bristle. At best you'd have to spend some time explaining to them (as Jacobus did to me) that this connection was never intended, and never entered your head.

Bill, Bill, Bill…

'Sangreal' is a great name but 'Sodality' was a bad choice. 'Sod' as well you know, is a mild English insult, though not originally connected with 'sodomy'. In certain contexts it does have connotations with the Earth, which is always good.

But… even though you've gone out of your way to deny any Nazi sympathies of any kind, 'S.S'. always always **ALWAYS** invokes the **S**chutz**S**taffel of the Nazi party.

There, I've said it at last.

I don't actually enjoy talking about 'occult' things except with Margaret, though I'm quite happy to listen to gossip or yarns. David Conway is good for the gossip, Dolores the yarns. And Laura Jennings told me many wonderful things, including the one about the woman in her GD group who gave 'old Regardie' a mercy blow-job when they arranged to give him the Adeptus Minor initiation he never did achieve in his youth, for all the noises made. I mentioned a few more bits of gossip about Doreen and Sanders and a host of others in the first draft of this but seeing them all in cold black and white text makes it look tawdry and dated.

Quite pitiful, really. I really must get out more. Where's David Conway when I need him?

No Bill, we really wouldn't get on in the flesh these days.

But God Bless you – and Bobbie – anyway…

Alan

Wm. G. Gray
14. Bennington St.
Cheltenham
Glos. GL50 4ED

Telephone

(0242) 24129

6 SEPT 1987

Dear Alan,

Thanks for your note with new address, and greetings to your new baby. Bless her.

My autobiography is firmly refused by Weisers on the grounds of no interest to them or anyone else. Jacobus has it in South Africa at the moment. He is reputed to be bringing out the Bloodmother himself, but I haven't heard a word for months. Weisers will be bringing out my Sangreal Tarot any time between Xmas and the next fifty years. I've just done my book on Satanism, and Llewellyns have taken a book on ritual procedures which Weisers turned down, but of course they never pay royalties. Still it might as well be circulating as chucked in my dustbin.

I'm just getting old and weary and not much else I'm afraid. It takes me ages to do a typescript, but this is the last book I m attempting in this incarnation. What are you working on at the moment?

To be perfectly truthful, I've got an idea I've met Dion Fortune's reincarnation in the States. If it isn't, she's a damn good imitation, even to size, hair colour, and <u>nature</u>. Not nearly so emphatic though, but the firmness is all there and so is the determination. I haven't told her what I think, because I might be wrong, but she has this feeling that Fortune's books ought to be rewritten and she can't think why!!!! I've not said a word. She'd like me to go back next year but God knows if I'll get anywhere except the boneyard.

Anyway, good luck, Bobbie says to remember her kindly, God Bless and KQ.

Bill

Garden Office   April 2nd 2023

Hello Bill!

New baby is Kirsty. I suspect she might be Herne's Child, for lots of reasons and non-reasons, but I know that other magickal parents have projected all sorts of things on their offspring and been greatly disappointed (and ultimately relieved) that they grew up into perfectly normal human beings. Kirsty will never disappoint me in any way or any reason at any level.

Llewellyns always paid *me* promptly. Never had any problem with them. Or any of the others come to think of it, except Thoth Publications. It's just that my books never sell in quantity, as I've moaned before. You'd think that my *Aleister Crowley and Dion Fortune – Logos of the Aeon & Shakti of the Age* might have been different but my total sales since publication in 2009 are - let me poke around for a moment and see...

BLOODY HELL...

The Guides or Whatever are now really taking the piss! I swear to god that at the **very moment** I wrote that sentence above, I received an email from Larry Kunkel of Llewellyn with a royalty statement!!!!

Perhaps it's the egregore of Llewellyns butting in to dispute your comments. Or even the owner, the late Carl Weschke, whom I met and liked and once showed around the Limpley Stoke Valley.

Llewellyn have always done their best for me, and been prompt with royalties. It's just my own style doesn't seem to click with the mass market. Maybe when I'm dead I might get the literary equivalent of Howard Carter to chisel through ancient walls of disinterest and discover me.

So... FYI...

Cumulative sales since publication in 2009 are 3,326. Plus 334 e-books. Given that it's now OOP, royalties from e-book sales this last year come to $1.36.

And that, Bill, is **my** all-time best-seller.

How strange, the timing of this.

I do sometimes wonder if They – whatever They are - take the piss. If they are aspects of mySelf, then I wish they'd turn Their energies into something useful. I've got this theory that They don't understand the numerical concept of Zero. So it's no use trying to invoke £1,000,000 because They will only end up gifting me £1 from a scratch-card.

Right then Bill…while They're in this mood, get to work. Have a word with the Inners and persuade Them to send me and Margaret a *very* large sum of dosh without hurting anyone, or impoverishing anyone. No tricks! We will do Good Things with it, and not tell a soul.

Oh and by the way, while we're on the topic of reincarnation of peoples in the States… the woman who insisted she was your mother in your next incarnation later wrote and told me that Bobbie had also been reborn there, as your little sister. She sent me photos of both, but I've deliberately lost them. I make no judgement here. This was not Marcia, incidentally.

As your comment about your forthcoming or stalled books, I will simply say this…

If I had to recommend any one book to a beginner who wanted to practice *real* Magic, then it would be your *Magical Ritual Methods*. The techniques have been stolen from it without acknowledgement a million times, largely by the Wiccans who exasperated you so much. I myself still find something new in it every time I look inside. It is brilliant, and years ahead of its time – the chapter on Ritual Sonics in particular.

A second book? Actually, it wouldn't be one by you. It would have to be Olive Pixley's *Armour of Light*, that I think Basil Wilby republished when he ran Helios Press. Unlike yours, the techniques given in *AoL* are exquisitely odd, curious, illogical - yet undeniably powerful. I've known senior Adepts make use of her techniques during the various times they feel 'stuck', as happens to everyone. Bizarrely (or perhaps not?) I found myself next to her brother's War Grave in Ypres, so I stood for a while and 'did the polite' as Miss Firth might have said.

Well, the Solar Flare doesn't seem to smashed into Wiltshire in any obvious way, but it's pissing down.

Alan

Wm. G. Gray
14. Bennington St.
Cheltenham
Glos. GL50 4ED

Telephone

(0242) 24129

17 October 1987

Dear Alan,

I've recently had a call from Jacobus who tells me that he has sent or is sending you the Typescript of my autobiography plus a letter which I hope you'll answer because he's rather an admirer of your work and sells it in his shop, I've seen it there myself. He is however a rotten correspondent, and I've only hard about two letters from him since I saw him last this March. But he's been ill a lot since I gather.

At last I've heard from people in London who think they might be going to start up a small Sangreal Temple, and I went up to meet them last weekend. Mainly a young and pleasant married couple plus a man about 40 connected with Basil Wilby's lot which he doesn't care for. Tells me that Basil has now gone all Buddhist and he feels he should be preferably connected with his own Western Inner Tradition. Anyway they are all sorting it out between them. I showed them the pictures of the other Temples just to prove they aren't the only ones, and they were quite impressed.

Then darned if I didn't get an enquiry from Wolverhampton from another bod a couple of days ago. Oh I knew the UK would be the last place to show interest in the SANGREAL Concept, but I didn't expect it much before the next century.

It wouldn't surprise me at all if Marcia. Pickands is Dion Fortune reincarnated. She's exactly like her in many ways except for the two kids.

My Bloodmother book that Jacobus is supposed to be producing isn't doing well at all. He is typesetting the thing himself apparently and swears it is being beautifully done, BUT its not the letterpress I'm worried about, but the finished shelf appearance. If he can get that done professionally it _might_ be OK, But if it doesn't look right that's the end of it. Anyway, we'll argue it all out IF I can manage to visit South Africa again, which I'm very uncertain about at the moment. I just want to concentrate on getting this thing going somewhere in London before I quit this world, anal then they can take over from me entirely.

Bobbie should get her bottom set of teeth in about a fortnights time if all goes well. The thrush-condition is nearly cleared, but not yet quite. They did warn her it would take a good many months to clear, My varicose ulcers on the right leg are very considerably improved, but not yet finished.

I came across a derivation of the word SANGREAL suggested as the French phrase *a son gre*. Meaning "at his will, pleasure, desire, etc".I suppose you could put it "What You Will" or even "Thy Will be Done", or maybe "AS THOU WILT". All stemming from the idea that the SANGREAL as the "Holy Grail" supplied whatever suited anyone best.

I can't say this presumed derivation impresses me very much, but what interests me is <u>why</u> any writer should be so anxious to suppress any connection with Blood. How they can possibly make <u>Sang</u> mean anything else? There was also a suggestion that the Lapis Exilis derived from "ex coelis" or "from Heaven". But surely our Satan came from there too???? God preserve me from wordsmiths! Far more likely the Exiled Stone was either a massive meteorite or a crashing Spaceship as that mentioned in the Book of Enoch or hinted at in the Biblical account of the Ten Commandments episode studied carefully in the light of modern possibilities. Oh I think that Von Danniken had something with his SpaceGod theories, but I do prefer the Book of Enoch presentation.

Anyhow I do hope the autobiog gets to you safely, but remember it's only a Draft copy. I wasted a whole year on it and Weisers rejected it sight unseen. Let me know if the packet gets to you.

Bill

Leyker's   3rd April 2023

Dear Bill,

My heart is rather sinking at reading your last, because I know that none of the Temples you have high hopes for will take off, and the one that does get established seemed to fall apart quite quickly due to internal stresses among the initiates.

I still can't sink my thoughts into your Sangreal Concept. But if anyone ever reads what is now our joint, weirdly-co-written manuscript, I'm sure at least one of them will leap with delight and get it *exactly*. So perhaps this whole project is meant for them, somehow. No doubt they'll then lambast me for being a magickal moron, or spiritually stupid or divinely daft. I say this because I've *just* remembered that you liked using alliterations; you felt that this technique embedded the words and concepts in people's minds. I suppose it worked to some degree, as whenever anyone talked to me about 'WGG' they often mention your 'Perfect Peace Profound…' And their words always tail off as though they can get some sense of what that might feel like.

A bizarre thought just floated in, so I'll go with it… Did you ever see the series *Dad's Army*, about the Home Guard during the Second World War? It strikes me that in some ways, in the very early days of knowing you, I often played the gormless Private Pike to your curmudgeonly Captain Mainwaring. Actually Bill, you and the good Captain, as played by Arthur Lowe, were not dissimilar in appearance. Whereas I was (and am) physically pretty much of a doppelganger for Pike, whose slowness and idiocy often provoked the magisterial comment: *Stupid Boy!* The difference now being that I'd consider myself a Lieutenant Colonel at least.

Oh but my thoughts perk up at your mention of the 'SpaceGod theories'! I do remember in the autumn of 1973, when I was still a Bright Young Thing in your eyes, you telling me that our origins are extra-terrestrial. This was long long before Erich von Daniken's *Chariots of the Gods* which, for all is obvious faults, opened the doors to all sorts of ponderings. As I recall though, you didn't attribute all this to rocket-powered space-ships as Daniken did. I think you suggested that these extra-terrestrials were more akin to space-born viruses than anything relying upon nuts and bolts and warp drives. I might be wrong.

I've actually just used my own version of the Akashic Records (ie Google) and looked up what you once said in Volume 1 of the *Sangreal Series*. I've got a signed copy in my own Upper Room but I'm a bit weary today, and somewhat despondent about my own health battles, so I'm taking the lazy man's approach and looking this up on my phone. And there it is, free for anyone to view on the 'Internet Archive', in the section on the Catechism...

'Esoteric teaching says that it [human life] began with inter-breeding between anthropoid humans and a far superior race from another solar system many millennia ago.'

With what result, Bill?

'...the ever-widening dissemination of the Sangreal strain among its peoples on this planet, which has considerably influenced our civilisation's culture for the better. It has inculcated an unusual element of true self-sacrifice among its human holders.'

So there we have it, from your point of view.

I must confess, that years before I looked at this Second Tranche, I'd been fascinated by the whole Alternative History of the pre-Sumerians and the Annunaki, as detailed by (among others) Zecharia Sitchin. According to him, using translations of Sumerian texts, the Annunaki was a race of extraterrestrials from a planet beyond Neptune called *Nibiru*. Also according to him, the interbreeding that you mention Bill (decades before Sitkin's stuff), began with the primitive proto-beings in deepest Africa, where the Annunaki created a new slave-race that they used as gold miners once they grew to adulthood.

Of course the academics completely tore his books apart, describing all this as psuedo-history. (Rather like the Old and New Testaments I suppose.) But I don't worry about that. In fact I'm quite happy to 'go with the flow', suspending disbelief as you do when watching something at a theatre. It's far more exciting than that bloody Grail of yours. The only thing I can't accept is Sitchin writing about the Anunnaki using rocket-ships. They had to have had something better than that.

Alan

Wm. G. Gray
14. Bennington St.
Cheltenham
Glos. GL50 4ED

Telephone

(0242) 24129

?? October 1987

Dear Alan,

Thanks for your rapid reply. I've just, sent off a bit of a blast to Jacobus knowing his unreliability regarding mail. You should get the manuscript <u>eventually</u> because there are two photocopies drifting around...

I note Dion Fortune's "Avalon of the Heart" has just come out again simply as "Glastonbury", and I'm looking forward to going through it again just to pick the lumps out so to speak. For instance that bit about the "finding of the Grail". That <u>was</u> a strange story which I can only think of as a glorious Cosmic joke, but the thing does exist and is still in the "Upper Room" in "Little St Michaels". I don't know know what you've heard, but the facts as I know them are roughly as follows...

Maybe some fifty years ago this chap whose name I've forgotten went on holiday to Italy, and as a curio bought this dish-like piece of work. Returning to home near Glastonbury he kept getting this dream suggesting he threw the item into Saint Bride's well (now concreted over). Anyway it wasn't a valuable piece and the dream kept pestering, so he did just that and hoped it would bring some luck, Believe it or not, a bit later on Mrs Sandeman (of Sandeman Port no less) then began to dream she should look for the Holy Grail in St Bride's Well. Again the dream nagged. So one day she and a friend, who might have been Diane Hope, went over to the well in bathing costumes (it was only some three or four feet deep) and grovelled around in the mud until triumphant hands encountered an unfamiliar object and up she came.

"HOLY GRAIL FOUND" the local papers were quick to announce with lots of ?????????s. (Of course the original owner then came forward and told <u>his</u> story. In fact the thing was just a nice piece of millefiore (thousands of flowers) work, possibly a century at most old and extremely common in Italy, Not valuable in the least on account of being too common even if pleasing, But the dream part IS true...

Anyway Tudor Pole (God rest his old soul) got hold of it at the Well, and I believe it's still there, Seems to show God (or whoever) has a sense of humour.

I haven't heard any more from the London people, but I believe they were going to make up their minds up in whose flat to start a Temple, so maybe I'll hear in the course of the next few clays, Purely for information, one of them is: [redacted by me]. He has contacts with Basil Wilby whom he doesn't like a lot, knows a few of the Inner Light lot, and the youngish married (or sex-mated) couple are: [redacted by me]. I liked them all personally so far as anyone can on initial encounters.

There's also a guy I don't know except on the phone who is advertising in "Prediction" for those interested in a Sangreal Temple. And I've recently had a bod writing from Wolverhampton. Another odd bod in the Bronx is thinking of starting up, plus some female in Wodstock NY which Marcia is looking' into.

No, I didn't know DF's mum was interested in running a commune, which was a fairly new thing in those days, although the Whiteways Colony is on our doorstep <u>here</u>, They started on Tolstoyan lines, and were really a Kibbutz of which there are endless numbers in Israel, and are now becoming an embarrassment to the Government, although they really got the whole of Israel going. We used to call them "Free Love Colonies" when I was in Palestine as it was then. But they're a story by themselves. Community living is normally monastic and has to run along those lines, But a "commune" is really the same system without any religion. Most of the kibbutzim are non-religious or describe themselves as "free thinkers", but they run themselves on very highly disciplined principles, That's they only way they <u>can</u> work.

Anyway, thanks for all the helpful comments. I didn't think for one moment the Sangreal Movement would do much in this country until the next century, but that's getting close now. Oh well,
          God Bless and KQ.

Bill

The Atrium   4th April 2023

Dear Bill,

I know that story about the GlasVegasbury Grail from St. Bride's Well. The best account is in *The Avalonians* by Patrick Benham. For some reason he mentions me in the dedication, but I can't remember what I might have contributed. I was still in awe of the Glastonbury 'Thing' then, so it wouldn't have been a sneer. I was young, remember.

As I think I mentioned earlier, some time before the Covid Lockdown, I met a woman from a Mediterranean land who was convinced *she* had written *Avalon of the Heart* in her previous incarnation. I met her at the Limpley Stoke Hotel, still known locally as the Hydro, that Violet Firth's parents and grandparents once ran, and gave her my famous tour of the Limpley Stoke Valley. DF's parents were married at the church of St. Mary the Virgin in Limpley Stoke, and my first visit there proved to be – coincidentally! – 100 years after that event. DF's maternal grandparents are buried in the churchyard. My erstwhile guest from a far-flung country felt the whole area was *leeminaal! leeminaal!*

Was *she* – is *she* – DF reborn?

Honestly Bill, I make no judgement.

As for the 'Cosmic Jokes' surrounding the incident of that particular Grail (and the library off to my right has at least half a dozen books identifying five other 'True' Grails), I do think that They often indulge in this. There's a Trickster element involved. But the 'jokes' – I speak from long experience here - are often sour. I think that everyone on what used to be called The Path is often taken up back-alleys and into magickal dead-ends, usually involving a series of serendipities and synchronicities of such complexity and unlikelihood that all seem to offer proof of their validity. Then everything dissolves at the last moment, like Faery Gold and you're left feeling exhausted, bewildered and sometimes a bit stupid. I can yarn more about this sort of thing than you.

As to the fate of your Sangreal Movement… I've been very tired lately, wrestling with my own health issues, so I haven't googled enough or tried to contact your god-son Marcus Claridge to see whether it survives and thrives. You can get pissy with me, but I suspect that it will turn out to be a piece of spiritual millefiore and won't make its first century.

And I'm quite sure that people will say the same thing about my own Work as something of a dead end.

Bah! At my age why moan?! I can't complain. I've had a grand sort of personal Quest and an amazing time of it while retaining all my own teeth, a full head of hair and most of my faculties. Once I get this new stone removed from near my bollocks (the first one nearly killed me), I'll be onward ever inward again. We rather hope to visit all the Magdalen Churches in Wiltshire, not for any specific purpose, but just to have a mild, undemanding mission that will involve picnics. I'd recommend that to everyone, finding the magick in the mundane.

It works for us...

alan

Wm. G. Gray
14. Bennington St.
Cheltenham
Glos. GL50 4ED

Telephone

(0242) 24129

31ˢᵗ OCT 1987

Dear Alan,

From what you say in your first few paras, wouldn't you suppose <u>something</u> of an important Concept is trying; (and apparently succeeding) to make a breakthrough into the Occidental or Wesoteric "Shared Subconsciousness" or whatever you prefer to call it.

I remember old Tudor Pole and his sweet little sister Kitty very well indeed and they were both very likeable people. Last time I saw him it was on Glastonbury Tor. He was on his own coming down and we (Bobbie and I) were going up. He waved his stick very cheerfully and shouted "Glorious day isn't it?" as we passed. He was a bit near ninety then. Kitty made 102 I believe. They used to call him just TP. Officially a Quaker, or Friend as they prefer to be called from their habit of calling everyone "Friend".

I note you've started the questions already so I'll clear up whatever I can as honestly as possible.

Yes the legend went that Michael knocked a huge emerald out of Lucifer's crown which fell to earth before he did and became one of two things or possibly both. The famous Smaragdine Table of Hermes reputed to have been found in the Great Pyramid, (which is patently untrue) and/or the Holy Grail itself. Now if you take the name of this or its description to be Lapis Exilis, (Jewel of Exile) and suppose the phrase is really "ex coelis" (from Heaven) you can then do a bit more word-splitting and make it La pis, which is French for "The worse(t)" so that the whole phrase implies "The worst out of Heaven" and who or what would that be???? None other than our mutual friend Lucifer-Satan in person bless his horny hoofs, not to mention his hoofy horns. So does that make Satan the Sangreal? NO it does not, but it sets some thinking in motion. (Of course "The Old Dragon" was a common alternative for Satan, but remember the Dragon was always the banner or heraldic sign for a Leader in military matters, and in Chinese mythology dragons are supposed to be supernatural people capable of appearing under whatever form they pleased, including beautiful young women, and their rank depended on the number of their claws.

Your queries about my psychological state when meeting people interested in forming a Sangreal Sodality group… I suppose one could describe it as "hopeful suspicion" based on past experiences. I suppose… after 75 years experience of humanity, I have serious doubts about my fellow-creatures efficacy in any solid spiritual way, which of course means my own as well. I suppose my attitude is similar to that of a bishop when queried about the authenticity of the Lourdes phenomena and was asked what he meant to do about it. In effect he said, "Nothing whatsoever. IF this is genuinely Our Lady, she will do it herself and nothing we can do will stop her, If however this should be a trick of Satan or a false belief it will die a natural death by itself, and we shall hear no more about it. So I'm waiting to see what happens."

Well that's more or less my attitude, with the Sangreal. All I've done is my part of the job and IF the Sangreal is capable of carrying on by itself, than let it do so and I'm willing to help however I can. I take it for granted that opposition to it is bound to occur, and in fact if it didn't, I would be more suspicious than ever. What is better evidence of Good than Evil? Or evidence of Evil than Good for that matter? Only polarities make Power possible.

No, I <u>don't</u> know the names of my Inners or even if they have names, It would be easy enough to assign them names, and I sometimes wonder should I have done so, but its a bit late in life to start now. They could only be substitute-names anyway, All I actually know is that there <u>are</u> Inners, but what I would query is my own personal relationship with them. And no again, I don't "go inside" after meeting the London people and ask the Inners' opinion of them...

Where did you contact Ron Heaver or hear about him? He had a place at Kenton Mandeville in Somerset, and was quite a remarkable man. We met him years gone by, as "Zadok", a cripple from what they used to call infantile paralysis caught from swimming in a French river while an RAF pilot in WW 1. Looked after by his cousin Polly. He had converted an old dairy at the back of his property into a Temple which had an absolutely <u>amazing</u> atmosphere. Hardly anything in it at all, but I remember a mantelpiece being an altar on which was a handsome Celtic

Cross, an English Prayer Book, and of all things a Tibetan dorje. Rush bottomed chairs, and rush matting on the floor. Plain whitewashed walls and that was it. But the atmosphere was so powerful it felt like a huge cathedral, which it probably was from an Inner point of view. He had a white cat which he swore was the same one who had been with him through three separate bodies. What is Zadok doing around your consciousness? He could only do something helpful or useful anyway. He died a long while back I'm afraid, and I never saved any of his letters.

I've not heard a toot from the London people since I saw them, so I'm wondering if they just said "yuck" and wrote me off as a bad bet...

Jacobus tells me that the Bloodmother book will probably be produced professionally in <u>Taiwan</u> just for the printing and production. They do an excellent job for less than half the price it would cost in South Africa. Of course that will add to the time quite considerably, but will at least produce something worth looking at in the shops. He already has an ISBN for it which he's sent me. He is thinking of redoing my Rollright Ritual under the new title of "Megalithic Magic" which I wrote a preface for a long while back...

Well, I guess that's about it for the moment, Let me know when that script arrives, and remember that if the worst ever came to the worst there are at least six other copies floating around South Africa, Also shoot your questions and I'll do my best to answer them as accurately as I can.

Godbless and KQ.

Bill

Garden Office – blistering sun!   5th April 2023

Dear Bill,
Am a bit knackered at the moment after attending my own weekly 'Coven'. That's the name I give my Cardiac Rehab class that has about 12 people in it. As we worked through the structured circuit training a portion of my mind was on your previous missive and its ponderings.

Yes I finally got the MS of your autobiography. Not sure who sent it. And thanks for that long letter. I've actually edited it slightly because it was filled with a healthy chattiness about mundane things, and lots of loving concern about Bobbie's health.

You asked: '...wouldn't you suppose *something* of an important Concept is trying; (and apparently succeeding) to make a breakthrough' into our shared subconsciousness.

Well... I suppose so. But what springs to my mind now is not the Sangreal but your mention of the Dragon. At that time I was working on a second batch of Christine Hartley's 'Magical Diaries' relating to the Work she did within the GD Temple of the Stella Matutina. These detailed some of her inner magick with Colonel Seymour, whom I told you about earlier. Once I'd finished that manuscript (then for some reason I'll always regret) I let Geoff Hughes add his own Diaries for his Work involving Dragon energies. The book was published by Llewellyns and given a stupid title (*Ancient Magick for a New Age*) and had an embarrassing cover filled with a Dragon. I hated it. I was naive, Bill. In those days I still thought that because Geoff was an initiate of the Inner Light, the very act of initiation there must have given him access to higher, supra-human wisdoms. I should have listened to you in that respect.

Geoff had raw power (though his wife Val was a far better psychic) but he went a bit daft. He felt – he *knew* – that he was the Merlin of Britain. I mean **the** Merlin of Britain. Rather like those women who have **known** that they were DF reborn. Perhaps, in both cases, because of some Concept trying to make a breakthrough into shared subconsciousness.

I did tell him that I knew several other magicians working the Merlin Current at that time. Including Basil Wilby. In fact I'd seen Basil in full flow of the Merlin archetype and that was quite something, even if the ritual itself was branded as disastrous by many others present. Geoff was jealous of Basil. Geoff was having visions of the US Superbowl filled with 100,000 adoring followers there for him alone, chanting: *Geoffrey, Geoffrey, Geoffreeeey...* 'It will happen Alan, I *know*.'

Of course it didn't. As I said in my previous letters to you there were endless synchronicities during this time as 'some Concept' seemed to be trying to make a point. Eventually I had to break off all contact with him. He gave up his job thinking that the royalties were going to make him rich – rich enough to tour the country lecturing/channelling as the True Merlin. I warned him to expect no more than perhaps £100 split 50/50 but he laughed. I'm not even sure if we got that much.

I don't feel smug remembering all that. All I know is that he and Val divorced and I heard that he died a couple of years ago.

I wish I could say, or see in retrospect, that your own 'Important Concept' of the Sangreal Sodality really was sneaking into the Collective Consciousness. Perhaps it did. I keep pretty much apart from the outer world of 'occultism'. It's quite possible that there was tidal wave from the inner planes that has now become mainstream, and I just haven't been aware.

But as I write that, I get a pop-up from the splendidly-entitled 'Keepers of the Planetary Flame' - always posted with the brackets (Gareth Knight) following. It says: 'Some believe that the Equinox is the beginning of a new era of humanity, where some of us feel more connected with our star lineage.'

I dare say you would go along with that if the dreaded GK wasn't connected. I'm sure you will say that 'star lineage' and 'blood lineage' are one and the same.

Perhaps they are...

Alan

Wm. G. Gray
14. Bennington St.
Cheltenham
Glos. GL50 4ED

Telephone

(0242) 24129

19 Dec 1987

Dear Alan,

Glad you enjoyed the autobiog…. ENH was Emil Napoleon Hauenstein, an Austrian who had been over here for years and contacted me because of a letter I'd written to the Occult Review ref the Rosicrucians. He had been a member of Papus' organisation, and subsequently the AMORC, which I've disliked all my life. As you probably know they were started up by an American salesman Spencer Lewis who eventually made vast sums of money out of them. The point was that ENH took over a lot of expertise with him which helped Lewis get his act together, yet in the end he had to admit what a swindle it all was and very quietly quit the organisation. ENH was also a Martinist of a very Christian variety. He was a Chef of the very top quality such as the Dorchester and so forth. Married very unfortunately, his wife going mad and living permanently in a nuthouse (Colney Hatch if I remember) and one daughter (Dorothy) who was living with her father. Since he never took out proper naturalisation papers he was interned during the war and subsequently died of cancer of the liver. My own belief was that formerly he had been Eliphas Levi, and my own mother had been his estranged ex-wife, Noemie Cadiot - but that is <u>purely private</u> and not to be mentioned... In which case he would have been born shortly after Levi's death and my mother not a very long time later.

    Dion Fortune and I did not have any very close relationships with each other apart from the little I mentioned, although I was aware of her influence with my Talking Tree book, sporadic as it might have been. I believe we were conscious of each other at a distance so to speak, and we were certainly engaged on the same project of reconstituting the "Mass of the Mysteries" with which she produced a very Anglican version, whereas I brought out the Sangreal Sacrament, which you know. You would not believe the various things which went wrong with its publication. Rejected by every publisher all over the place, mucked about with by musicians who promised music for it, God knows what, till in the end I published it myself and it was actually Bob Stewart who got it professionally recorded at his place in Bath, and we made the original tapes from that. That was the one publication I was really concerned about, and once it was in circulation I felt I'd done my real lifework. It had taken me 50 years on and off.

Now so far as my "Inners" are concerned...

Are they often wrong? Frankly I don't know, but I know I am often wrong in interpreting their communications. How do I "get in touch?" Again I don't know. Sometimes I am conscious of a kind of "presence" more or less just behind me somewhat to my left, (the receptive side), or of course that could be my left brain activating itself. Phenomena? You mean PK stuff? None that I know of in that sense at all, although I believe I've mentioned most of the little incidents inclining me to believe in occasional contacts between our world and some "Otherwhere" you can put any name you like to. Do I know who these Inners are? No, not by any names which might be familiar. And do I trust them? Not by one single inch so far as my person is concerned.

They aren't interested in doing anything for me, but with me if you get the difference, so you might say we have a love-hate relationship. What are they? I suppose the same ones who are concerned with perpetuating the Wesoteric Tradition in this world through anybody they can get hold of who is willing to do the work in whichever field they specialise, which would mean the same ones who influence you among others.

So if it boils down to brass tacks, who IS behind our Western Way as distinct from say Oriental or other spiritual systems within this world? The usual mysterious "They" so commonly quoted by most of the masses blaming "Them" for about everything in creation. Does anybody actually know the relatively few individuals responsible for our so-called civilisation? I don't mean the public politicians, but the "behind the scene" boys and girls who pull the strings of the puppets on the world-stage? (Which is one of the reasons I like the "Spitting Image" TV thing.) I am more concerned with those who pull the strings of our "unknown owners" invisibly from a suspected yet non-evident condition of consciousness behind our beings.

You may remember the Rosicrucians once called this their "Invisible Government" though what made them think it might be better than their visible one is a mystery. That was probably just wishful thinking or hopeful projections of some kind. Do any of us ever know just who or what is pulling our strings from some unknown (as yet) Inner Dimension?

    No, I don't believe the Sangreal Sodality concept will ever make anything of itself in Britain, mostly because of sheer lack of interest… The people I met in London were a complete waste of time. On the surface there was nothing to make a fuss about. The leader [N.] gave me the impression of being unstable, but seemed an otherwise likeable person. Yet after a disgraceful and total volte face, entirely unexpectedly and inexplicably, I've told him in no uncertain terms to go to Hell as quickly as he likes.

Bill

The Atrium   April 5th 2023

Today is a perfect day. Putin hasn't yet obliterated the world and the U3A are gathered en masse again, unbowed, ready to march on out like pilgrims on a Crusade against Ageing. There are only two men among them, but I suspect that's coz women live longer than men. When I worked with my Mobile Library for the elderly I had very few men readers, and very many widows.

Yes Bill, I did enjoy your autobiog. There were many sections that were compelling and quite brilliant, but others that varied between the mundane and malign. It should have been an increasingly triumphant journey toward the glory of your Sangreal Revelation, but in crucial places it went bland. Almost as though your soul was resting in some formless Bardo before you get to the Clear White Light and go forever onward. Your description of your time in South Africa should have been the climax, but it was almost like a schoolboy essay of 'What I did in the Holidays'.

That was the *real* reason that Weiser and Llewellyns backed out of publication. It lacked the *oomph* of million-sellers like 'To Ride a Silver Broomstick'. I know, I know, I bloody know! Stupid title, stupid book, but that's what the punters want. Don't get me started on that one. Of course I'm truly, madly, deeply jealous.

Ironically, if you'd sold a meaty tale about your magic with Pat Crowther and Doreen Valiente (now seen as the Founding Mothers of modern Witchcraft) and the uncanny but intriguing Robert Cochrane, you'd have had a modest best-seller. You wouldn't even have had to pose naked with a towel around your waist, while Pat Crowther, by her own admission, always loved getting her kecks off for the tabloids. That's what they wanted. *Wicca wicca wicca. Witch witch witch...*

So, Bill, I know this because those publishers told me personally that your autobiog required too much work. It would have required lengthy and judicious editing by some mug(s) willing to toil away and craft it without any likelihood of reward and little likelihood of sales. Where would you find *anyone* daft enough for that? Actually, it took some ten years before me and your godson Marcus Claridge did exactly this, with the encouragement of Suzanne Ruthven who ran the tiny indie *ignotus press*. It was she who brought out the first edition of *The Old Sod* – a title that Jacobus *hated*. But bollocks to him, as we all felt.

As I don't have Marcus's email and don't like phones (I'm somewhat hearing-impaired) I wrote him a brief old-fashioned letter only yesterday asking if he knew anything about the Bloodmother. When I first met you, it was possible to dine out on the cost of a first class stamp today. And you *always* used a *first* class stamp when dealing with any magical matter, so I did the same as an act of *homage*, as the French would say.

We'll see where this might take me.

AMORC... They had a branch which met in a hotel in Newcastle. When I was 16ish I took the bus there from Ashington, using up my pocket money for the fare. I waited around the doorstep for a couple of hours hoping to see what I imagined would be *real* Adepts entering. As it was, no-one turned up, but I don't know what I would have said if they had. They might have thought I was a rent-boy! It started raining so I went off to an aeromodelling shop further up the street and bought a glider. I still believed everything I read in AMORC's glossy pamphlets and didn't understand, or couldn't accept, that people can tell both harmless, glamorous fibs (as I've often done myself), or blatant but persuasive and dangerous lies. I think I've avoided any of the latter - but then again I might be fibbing about that.

I totally agree with your assessment of AMORC. I knew a fella who became as disillusioned by them as ENH.

The Inners...

As you know, due in no small part to your clairvoyance, I managed to wangle funding for a scholarship at the University of Kentucky in 1974 – long after you'd banished me from your place in 'Nam. There, I met a fella my age who was deeply into Magic – without the 'k'. And pretty much without anything else as far as I could sense. Bill McSomething. Handsome lad, wealthy. Gorgeous girlfriend. His whole large apartment was made into a private Temple, with hand-painted kabbalistic symbols and Trees of Life in appropriate places, but the whole place felt dead. I mentioned your name. He'd read one of your books. I asked him about *his* Inners and he was bewildered. What Inners? I mentioned that you had had psychic contact with DF. He thought the whole notion absurd, and was embarrassed for me that I'd even accepted the likelihood of 'Inners'. I didn't bother debating the issue. I've sometimes wondered if he ever found his way Inward, or if he became like Spencer Lewis and created his own, money-spinning version of AMORC. He had charisma. I'm sure he'd make a fortune.

But I pounce upon your comment: "I know I am often wrong in interpreting Their communications."

That line is important!

You see I've promised to meet an American lad in the nearby and highly magickal town of Frome next month, who insists that he has *always* wanted to meet me. I'll take him up to the café in the Rye Bakery and chat there, manipulating him onto the side of my one good-ish ear. I'm rather anxious, because he wants to meet 'Alan Richardson' but there's no such being. (I really *should* have used a pen-name like Basil did.) This fella has read everything I've written about you and has published some of it in his magazine. But it's not your Sangreal stuff that excites him…It was your involvement with the witches that energised *his* inner stuff.

Perhaps every magical Working is more effective in the unexpected and usually unintended consequences, than in the immediate visions? I know that stuff I did in my teens aiming for Pan, that seemed to be ineffective at the time, manifested decades later in ways that I would never have imagined or expected.

Anyway, I'll do my best to inform and entertain the lad, then like the old *News of the World* reporters I'll 'make my excuses and leave'. I've been doing that sort of thing for a looooong time now Bill...

alan

Wm. G. Gray
14. Bennington St.
Cheltenham
Glos. GL50 4ED

Telephone

(0242) 24129

13 JAN 1988

Dear Alan,

I've been going over the book about Regardie that you sent me and its almost brought the old boy back to life for me for a few moments. Just as I knew him, God rest his rebellious old soul. He'll be bouncing back again in no time somewhere if not already. Yet why the hell he never mentioned the Crowley happening with the servant-girl in that book, I'm damned if I know. Maybe he thought it was widely known.

I'd support a very great deal of what he said BUT he was specifically referring to a "general" class of occultist which _are_ in fact dilettante and ineffective. Carr Collins was one such, and yet from other viewpoints he was, as Regardie said, a wholly delightful and loveable individual. I suppose you could say that he _did_ something by subsidising all my work with Weisers. Do you know I wouldn't have got _anything_ accepted otherwise? They won't touch anything I've done since Carr died.

Nevertheless Regardie was right about the "Sweetness and Light" brigade being so useless and inconsequential, but I don't believe he'd thought it all through properly. OK, so they're the "tepids" which so annoyed Jesus, the "wishy-washies" and the "perhaps-people" who never seem to do to do anything much except get in the way of those who are trying to accomplish _something_ in the field, so to speak. Nevertheless they DO have a purpose, being the sort of "filling" or inert and inactive material which forms a kind of "bulk" to our spiritual structure as it were. They just aren't the _active_ ingredients of the mixture so to speak, but the passive, apparently purposeless, and just inoperative class of people who make up the "mass" of _any_ human society, yet _without_ them, the vitalising few couldn't even exist. I don't think Regardie ever quite appreciated that. It's taken me about a whole lifetime to see the necessity for quite a lot of what I once thought useless and pointless annoyances.

And your note today. A Mithraic connection! Funny how that relatively obscure sect from Persia caught on in the Roman Army. It was rather a Masonic thing in a way, and strictly speaking a sort of "Friendly Society" with sick-benefits, burial fees, and all kinds of social insurance available to members depending on rank etc. It wasn't so much religious as plain humanitarian in nature, and had it been inclusive of women or had a wider interpretation it would have been the popular socio-religious cult of the West instead of Christianity. Sure it would have needed all sorts of secretaries and accountants to administer its funds and disbursements. It didn't have what I would have called real priests. Above a certain grade about every officer took their turn at ceremonial duties, but in order to belong in the first place, you had to be reliable and of proven honesty and integrity. The mythos behind the cult itself was of great antiquity yet supreme simplicity, The young warrior-hero who provides food for his kinsfolk at the cost of his own life, all linked with blood. One might call it the very essence of esotericism. Virtually our oldest form of Sacred-Kin(g)ship. (In Mithraism, symbolised by the blood-baptism of the tauroboleum.) Can't you hear all the controversy between the Mithraics and the Christians concerning what the former would call real baptism with genuine blood, while the latter were satisfied with the weaker substitution of water, though to this day they talk about the "Blood of the Lamb" and still claim it was the blood of Jesus which was supposed to have saved the whole world. Mind you, that blood-initiation with a whole bull was a hell of an expensive business and God alone knows how long a Lodge had to save up in order to make one possible, The initiate was supposed to pay for a lot of it, and of course the whole Group had beefburgers for ages afterwards, but even so an initiation wasn't an everyday occurrence by any means…

You might have noticed, by the way, that old Regardie in his forebodings had a particular interest that as much of our Western Inner Tradition as possible might be established in the Southern Hemisphere so that it would continue after the climactic or other disasters had overtaken what is now our Western World. Bobbie has always felt that this is the reason I've never had the slightest success with any attempts at getting any kind of Sangreal Sodality started in the UK, and yet it's taking off in South America, South Africa and even the States. Mind you, I've seen about five reputed "end of the worlds" during my lifetime... This coming disaster is supposed to be in the 1990's which is almost upon us...

At any rate I've had a great deal of enjoyment out of your Regardie book purely because of my personal contacts with the man, and I grant you it mightn't mean a lot to someone who hadn't known any of that crowd. For all I know your friend Simon Buxton might look at me as a boring old has-been who didn't know his arse from his athame, or something equally hopeless and outdated. After all, I'm not exactly a popular sort of person and quite a few would look at my Sangreal Concept as being a recrudescence of the Nazi blood-Idea, linking it with Satanic rites of the worst kind plus God alone knows what nastiness, for absolutely no solid reason whatsoever apart from the fact they don't <u>want</u> to know. Don't forget I've known of Nonconformists who genuinely don't believe Catholics can possibly be Christians of any sort and firmly believe they worship the Virgin Mary alone... I've been a pretty unpopular character with quite a lot of occult types at whose feet I would not care to worship, but do always remember I've never made the slightest claim in any esoteric direction as regards my individual self. All I've done is to try and elucidate the spirit of our Western Inner Tradition as I've encountered it and as I hope other humans will develop and carry it along ever-improving lines.

Anyway I'll get this off now and shift some more correspondence. I couldn't help thinking how odd it was that both Regardie and Gerald Gardner should drop dead at breakfast – quite happily. My father died while getting his breakfast and I'm sure his last thought was: "Damn. I didn't feed Happy." (his cat)

Still nothing from Jacobus of course...

Bill

Limpley Stoke Hotel   March 7th 2023

Hello Bill,

A glorious and sunny day today so far. I'm scribbling this on the patio of the LS Hotel which is a something of a spiritual nexus for me, despite its outward veneer of staid post-Victorian solidity. Yet I've noticed for the first time a carving on the westward wall simply showing a cursive 1625. This building is nowhere near that age. What happened then, that it needed to be carved? The dreadful papist monarch Charles I came to the throne, believing in the Divine Right of Kings - which was his own version of the later and even more ridiculous Papal Infallibility. Anything else? Perhaps if I could stroke the stone numbers I might get ideas. The carving is bothering me, but it's too high for me to reach.

It makes me think of Robert Cochrane's group that you did magic with, and his emphasis on 1735, which apparently wasn't a year, but a code. I must google that later at home. Can't get a signal here in the valley.

You see I believe that *everything* can be seen as magickal event. And I'll try to use the word 'magic' instead of 'magick' for your sake. Of course you'd have to be pretty secure as an individual not to be driven loopy by this sort of thing, but I **am** secure. Am I loopy? I'll ask Margaret who's sitting next to me soaking in the sun and reading a posh magazine. She says **No**.

What happened to that group? I know that all the original members, many of whom I knew very slightly, are long since dead, but did it survive in any form? I feel a worm-hole opening as the waiter brings us tea and biscuits. C*lose close close my brow.*

However… I cut a lot of your previous letter down because it was long, amiable, whimsical even, and chatty. To get to the core… I can't remember sending you a book about Regardie. It couldn't have been very good, as I've always regretted loaning someone my copy of his excellent and now hugely expensive 'Eye in the Triangle', never to be seen again. I think it may have been one that Gerald Suster wrote and gave me. I met him when he and Laura Jennings visited me at Murhill. He was in the depths of his self-admitted alcoholism at the time. For some reason I can't watch heavy, mad drinking expressed on the telly, even in a fictional programme. I don't know why. My parents never had a problem. Perhaps this is a past life thing? As Judy Hall opined, sometimes reincarnation is the *only* possible explanation for certain things that affect us.

I liked your comments on Mithras. I know that you and Bobbie both felt that you had served in the XX Legion together, and I feel a similar connection. I know that a few units of this were based in Gloucester in the AD 50s. Perhaps that's why I was drawn there? I think that part of me *was* a priest, a Raven Priest, but as you say I/He/It/ was more of a civil servant than anything truly esoteric. As shown in Kim Seymour's Magical Diaries as published in my *Inner Realms of Christine Hartley,* I might have been the young Mithraic legionary he felt had a homo-erotic attachment to him.

I know you wouldn't be shocked by that, Bill. You have been branded a racist, because you actually were. A child of your times, like my parents and almost everyone of my parents generation. They didn't know any better. But you were never homophobic – unlike some of your contemporaries I could name. You wrote in a letter to Marcia before your falling out: "Still, I've always seen humans as being bi-sexual creations, their ultimate development auto-reproductive, though that's some millions of years away yet." You spoke fondly about an all male, homosexual coven you knew about. You would have no problem with the current Trans people, and would see them as evolutionary. But that's enough of that.

It's peaceful as I sit here. Margaret says it's bucolic, but that's an ugly word. I prefer Arcadian, with a sense of pan pipes from the nearby woods. The lambs are gambolling upon the hill that leads up to Winsley and the sky has circling crows, ready to swoop down and peck out their eyes given half a chance. Yet it's there in the valley and hill that my four daughters were conceived and grew up into magickal women, each one with their own special powers. Later on today we will take four of our grandchildren for a spectacular pizza at one of the many Italian places in this area - an echo of the Roman times again?

In a small way I get my own Perfect Peace Profound here. And a large pot of tea for two with a plate of biscuits, costs only £5.00. How can you ever move my sympathies toward the virtues of your Sangreal?

To quote yourself: "Not by one single inch so far as my person is concerned..."

Alan

Wm. G. Gray
14. Bennington St.
Cheltenham
Glos. GL50 4ED

Telephone

(0242) 24129

???

Dear Alan,

I thought I'd send you this because when dealing with Crowley you cannot overstress the importance of the incident of his mother catching him in bed with a servant girl, and her subsequent treatment of this, because that single occasion determined all the rest of his life and behaviour. Regardie never mentioned it in that book you sent, but this is what happened...

    As you may know, Crowley was brought up by hopelessly narrow-minded relatives of the Strict Plymouth Brethren persuasion. His father died when he was eight, and his mother went to live with an uncle nearly as narrow. Crowley was given no <u>personal</u> love at all, and was a naturally affectionate child with no means of expressing his emotions. When he came to sexual maturity his anxieties and suppressed feelings were beyond description. Apparently he had come to an understanding with the youngish "maid of all work" as they used to call them, that if ever an opportunity occurred she would initiate him into the delights of sexual experience. The uncle was apparently absent at the time, and one evening Mrs Crowley announced that she would be attending a religious meeting somewhere and would not be back until very late, but as she naturally had her own key, they need not wait up for her.

    That provided the opportunity needed, and so after a discreet interval, young Master Aleister and the girl (who was probably in the late twenties or so) decided to get together. They unwisely but understandably chose Mrs Crowley's big bed to perform in and indulged in considerable foreplay first. Eventually they got into the bed and commenced the serious business. Suddenly in virtual mid-bounce, the bedroom door opens and in came Mrs Crowley. The meeting had been cancelled at short notice...

    After her first horrified gasp, Mrs C ordered immediate cessation of such a shocking performance. The maid was sacked immediately and dismissed with no wages due... and given an hour to pack her things and depart.

But here comes the horrifying part. Mrs Crowley did NOT lose her temper, rage, or otherwise emotionalise. It would have been a lot better if she had, but she didn't. Instead she took the line of What had she ever done to offend God so much that He had sent her such a <u>wicked</u> <u>wicked</u> <u>WICKED</u> son? She went on and on lecturing young Aleister concerning his sinful and <u>evil</u> act.

I was told that this went on for at least four hours, with the wretched youth forced to listen to every word and nothing to say in his own defence. She continued vilifying him in that cold hard voice with every appropriate scriptural quote she could think of, especially from Revelations, particularly mentioning the Great Beast, and the Scarlet Woman. In the end, young Aleister was told to spend the rest of the night on his knees praying for forgiveness, and sent away with no supper.

At least that is the story I had from my mother who had it from Victor Newberg, who presumably had it from Crowley himself. I feel that this totally <u>explains</u> Crowley. But whose was the greater sin - his for following a natural instinct, or his mothers for following an unnatural and cruel doctrine? Do bear in mind that poor Aleister hadn't even had an orgasm for this unusual but literal coitus interruptus. Now is it any wonder that he had an odd life? All my own mother did was to warn me about the various venereal diseases I could catch if I wasn't careful, and advise me on essential points of hygiene. I doubt if there are many mothers today who would act like Mrs Crowley, though there could be some left I suppose....

By the way, Sphere Books (branch of Penguins) have just published something by one Anthony Harris, claiming that Jesus was really a <u>woman </u>named Yeshu. He skates around all the awkward points like the circumcision, Jewish ritual baths the fact that Romans crucified their condemned <u>naked</u>, and such-like things, but burbles on about Mary Magdalen, the Cathars, Templars (whose mysterious head he claims was Yeshu herself), the Holy Shroud and indeed God alone knows what else. I would class this with the "Manna Machine" and "Sun Gods in Exile" for pure spoof value. Oh well. If <u>that</u> is publishable, anything is.

Bill

Garden Office   8th April 2023

Hello Bill,
It's brisk and sunny today and M is off for a walk on the nearby Salisbury Plain with a friend. Many of the highly obscure, tiny places that Dennis Wheatley used in his ridiculous but marvellous *The Devil Rides Out* actually exist in that area. I read that paperback when I was 13 and shivered with horror about the demons invoked in those damned, far-off hamlets. I hadn't yet been south of Tyne and simply assumed that while Wheatley's devils and the sabbats were totally real, the places were probably fictional. Imagine my delight as a 70 year-old when I re-read it again and realised that while the devils and the sabbats were totally fictional, the actual *places* – most of them isolated hamlets in or around Salisbury Plain – were very real. As I described in my book about the 'Red Lady of Paviland', I had known these places intimately without realising where and when I had first read their names.

So there was a quantum-ish thing going on there too, somehow. You actually knew Dennis Wheatley and always insisted her was a real shit. He knew fuck-all about *real* magic though, despite his best sellers.

Our garden is normally full of birds (and several times we've had a small hawk perch on our fence!) but there's no sign of them at the moment. The starlings normally go through the fat balls three a day but they're still untouched, as are the non-grow seeds in the feeder, and also the meal worms we leave out specially for the blackbird in his secret places beneath the tree that has a name I can never remember but has violet blossoms. Why? I take this personally.

You mention Regardie again and this brings a magpie-like fluttering of thoughts, drawn to any glittering ideas I can steal. I suppose it's apt that today is the 119th anniversary of the *Book of the Law* being 'received' by Crowley – or was it really through his wife Rose? I used to know every detail, but now... Chain of memories coming up here...

I found your address as a teen in an old copy of the *New Dimensions* quarterly magazine published by Basil Wilby, that often had articles by the mysterious Gareth Knight. You'd inserted a little advert saying you were happy to respond to any 'poignant queries'.

But what I also remember was that it contained an article by this 'Israel Regardie' about 'Occult Eugenics'. In truth I hadn't a clue what

'Eugenics' was, occult or otherwise, as I was still a virgin and had only hazy ideas about what went where and why. I remember nothing about its contents. I'd like to see that essay again, if only to sneer at it for being dated. I know that a lot of things were forced on people in the US in particular in that era – lobotomies and the like, to cure epilepsy. Were they also into eugenicising people – however that worked? I've no doubt the Brits were doing much the same but would have hidden their secrets deeper.

Perhaps you and 'old Regardie' were *both* children of your time.

And now I've got an email from Marcus, your godson. I remember a diorama you made for him when he was a toddler. It was in a glass case, probably an upturned fishtank, and comprised Roman soldiers on a battlefield, one on a chariot,. I'd had the same charioteer figure myself as a boy, and so you must have got it from a local toy shop. Marcus tells me that the *Bloodmother* was eventually published by Llewellyn's as *Evoking the Primal Goddess*. They always did have a habit of changing titles to meet what they saw was market demands. That's not a bad title but not as good as *Bloodmother*. He also tells me it was not your best.

I've looked on-line but won't buy. £30.00 at least, and my modest pension wouldn't justify that. So I looked at the reviews on Amazon and they're about the same as I get: a couple of good ones, far too many one-star stinkers. One critic informs that there's a lot about the Grail and 'alien insemination of the human race'. I ignore the former but actually accept the latter, thanks to the writings of Sitkin and others, although you seem to have got there before any of them. Another reviewer described it as a 'strange read' – which actually makes it my kind of book. A third critic feels that your thinking reads more like turn of the century (the 20th not the 21st), and puts your book in the same class as that one by Anthony Harris you just demolished - about the Female Jesus and just about every Mystery and conspiracy east of Sedona where Regardie lived out his life. Call me shallow, but I'd actually love to read *that* one. I take huge enjoyment from all Conspiracy Theories, as I do Westerns and Sci Fi movies. I'm a freak in that I can believe all of them and none of them at the same time. But Taylor Ellwood is kinder in her review, giving it 4 stars, and says: 'It's an interesting book which explores the divine feminine and Gray has some interesting theories and ideas. At times the book wanders a bit and I would take some of what he shares with a grain of salt, but its worth a reading and pondering because as always Gray makes you think.'

I suppose I sound churlish and treacherous Bill, yet I honestly don't see any of *my* books surviving beyond my death. But if just one reader will one day say something alike… 'As always, old Richardson makes you think', then I'll be happy.

Best

Alan

PS I've just peeked into the musty letters of this Second Tranche to see what I might be working on tomorrow. A clutch has fallen out together like a group of sky divers. I have to chuckle when I see that one of them includes a page from Crowley's unpublished Magical Diary for 1922. I expect you were given this by Gerald Yorke. I suppose this Easter Weekend is somehow in quantum cahoots with the Three Days of *Liber Al*'s reception.

Hmmmm… I'll have to see if William Breeze - 'Hymenaeus Beta' of the O.T.O. - will let me have permission to use this, as he seems to own the copyright.

Holy Hiatus

That's a term you used Bill, probably in your *Rite of Light* that I bought from Atlantis Bookshop, probably in 1977. It's a little red booklet of 40 pages; mine is signed by you and numbered 341. It's next to me now as I sit in the office, dipping into it for the time since I performed bits and pieces of it on a patio overlooking the Lyncombe Vale in Bath, when no-one else was around of course. I didn't do robes or have any of the other paraphernalia but I did shower and change into clean clothes specially chosen. I still don't do robes or have much in the way of paraphernalia. I'm not knocking this, but I've always cleaved toward Colonel Seymour's statement to Christine Hartley that you didn't need a Chalice when you've got cupped hands; you didn't need a wand when you've got a pointing finger. I'm sure I'm missing out a lot by not going the Full Monty, as they say, but it seems to work adequately for me. We had still not made contact again, and I know you would have bristled at the notion of me only doing 'parts of it'.

In many ways I prefer it to the clunking Sangreal stuff, and I liked your 'Calling in the Circle' that you modified from one of the Gnostic Chants. I think that's probably the bit I did then before my landlady June Hall-Hall appeared, wondered what I was up to, and got me to dig up half the garden to find a broken sewer pipe in return for a reduction in our rent.

My inner magpie is squawking and fluttering again... And so I'm remembering how once when you walked with me to the bus station in Cheltenham and we passed a nearby church. You muttered how it was a very 'Low' Church, not to your taste. I probably gave a sycophantic nod in agreement. But I had grown up in the coal-mining town of Ashington without ever attending *any* kind of church. No-one I knew then – adult or youth or child – *ever* went to church. I had no idea what made any of these places High or Low. So the sequences within your *Rite of Light* were always a bit too much for my taste when I did come to attempt them. And I know that Marcia also curtailed some of the tedious stuff (as she saw it) of the Sangreal Ceremonies. Do I hear you bristle?

This hiatus - a pause or break in continuity - is because I've looked through the next clutch of letters and decided that I would pick out the best paragraphs from them. There is a lot of amicable 'noise' and 'stuff of life' comments showing you to be kinder to me then than perhaps I'm being toward you today. There is the very long, unpublished 'porno piece', as you termed it, from Crowley's Magical Diary that I'll add at the very end of this book. And there are several gems of magickal insight, plus numerous complaints of varying intensity about: Me, Marcia, 'Wilby', Mike Jamieson (an erstwhile and disappointing member of your group whom I met at your funeral), and very many increasingly angry moans about Jacobus, your 'spiritual son'. *And* there are also a few paragraphs that don't do *you* any favours in today's world. I won't reproduce them. In fact I *might* burn them like Arthur Chichester did with Dion Fortune's personal papers after her death. So what follows are the bits and pieces that make me give a curious *Hmmmm* – which is the nearest sonic I can get to going *Om*...

Wm. G. Gray
14. Bennington St.
Cheltenham
Glos. GL50 4ED

Telephone

(0242) 24129

29 JUNE 1988

Dear Alan,

I remember the last time I met Carr Collins I had never known him so genuinely "upset" as though something had gone out of his life which he could never replace. Despite all my questioning, I could discover nothing more than it was something Regardie had said which was the cause of his depression. It could be of course that he had instinctively reacted with the bug which was to kill him a year later, just as in the case of Dion Fortune who might equally have subconsciously sensed the leukaemia which was to end her life many months later. In other words, Regardie probably only touched off something in Carr which was smouldering anyway. My impression was that Regardie had indicated that he had come to the conclusion that esoteric endeavours were only a waste of time, the Golden Dawn was nothing but amateur theatricals, and the whole lot was only a load of crap anyway. Or something to that effect. To sum it up Carr was disillusioned as I believe Dion Fortune was. And wasn't even Jesus said to have died crying "My God my God, why have you deserted me?" Its that kind of uncertainty one encounters at the end of a lifetime, Was it all worth it - or NOT? Who can possibly answer with infallible certainty however much hope may be extended in any direction??? In fact hope is all one has, and if _that_ goes it leaves a frightful hole in its place....

13 JULY 1988

Arthur Chichester was unbelievably stuffy and off-putting. I remember how he used to sit steepling his fingers like a stage lawyer and flexing them in time with his rather hard and pedantic style of speech. He was the _anti_ part of the interviewers, because the Inner Light always did their interviewing of prospective candidates in the old-fashioned Good-Guy Bad-Guy way, or pro and anti. The pro part was usually taken by a rather genial "colonel-y" type of chap whose name totally escapes me. He did the encouragement to join the Inner Light bit, while Chichester did the discouragement bit. Seeing that he was an Intelligence Officer in the Air Force during World War 2 you can see where he derived his technique from.

6 APRIL 1989

Thanks for yours of today strange to say I'll been thinking of you since some of your Golden Dawn friends from California (a Mrs Laura Jennings) have been writing me and saying how much they enjoyed staying with you last year and how they're hoping to revisit and hope to look me up when they come over early October this year. Also how much they're hoping I'll write some bits for their "housemag". She sent me some nice pics of their regalia since they hire the local Masonic Hall for their monthly meetings. To me their stuff looks terribly gloomy being mostly black and white. I wrote to put them off since I'm walking worse almost every day and don't feel I can cope with new people any longer. But I've put them in touch with Marcia since every contact helps, even though I don't see what good in modern times a mythos based on the iconography and nomenclature of Ancient Egypt can be. It isn't relevant any longer, although the Death and Afterlife Existence of a Man-God is only an earlier form of Christianity. Also their complicated degree system is surely outdated in our days. And I don't take kindly to their fixed charges for initiation at all, plus their $200 a year membership. She was telling me they didn't manage to visit Glastonbury at all because of the weather but loved the beautiful Cathedral at Bath. Does she mean the Abbey I asked, because I think those ghastly 18th century memorials ruin the place with their fulsome and irritating character lies, and I would be glad to see them all removed to some less public place…

12 APRIL 1988

Bobbie is rather fascinated by your remarks about her and Gwyn ap Nudd. Actually "Light, son of Darkness" signifying the old FIAT LUX or the well known Yang-Yin. It's just the old Celtic name for a Power of Eternal Alternation which like other cultures they personalised. Almost anything could be expected of him. As Day came out of Night, Life came out of Death, Yes came out of No, and so creation continued, and that was it. The Celts just put things their way which was their adaption of an older system.

In point of fact the whole damn thing developed out of that we now call shamanism. A sort of Nature Religion you might call it which arose from people's personal experiences and reactions with Nature Itself. This resulted in a response from specific humans causing a character-change that seemed to "set them apart" from their ordinary fellows and "make them special" so that they were considered to be priests or at least have what we would now call Psi-powers, or uncommon faculties such as telepathy, clairvoyance, and possibly healing. Eventually it became noticed this was becoming hereditary within familial lines. Once the connections had time to build up, definite establishments and power-structures began and "orthodox" faiths and religions instituted formal proceedings in constructed buildings. In time standard ceremonials were being handed from one generation to another down the centuries, but at the back of everything the old spontaneous experience persisted, and the "priesthood after the order of Melchizadek" became born. In other words those who had "attained" priesthood for several lives eventually got born with the knowledge and experience in their genes already, so that priesthood became an hereditary function. As for example the Cohens with the Jews or the Brahmins with the Hindus. I don't know what they mostly were among the Celts, but the "Oak-men" or Druids amongst then did tend to run in families.

However, the ancestral memories of the early experiences have always been there, and humans have called them out in hopes of reviving the old links with ancient times so that it may be said in the old words of Adam "My priesthood and my gift of prophecy shall He restore to me etc..." when speaking of the coming Crucifixion which the now Bishop of Durham is trying to devalue. People are now trying to re-create that Melchizadek experience for themselves, which was the reason why DF shoved it in their initiation service...

I think I've told you I believe Marcia is DF back again though of course I can't prove it but I've known both women in one life and such is my conviction. If you ever get a chance to meet Marcia do, although you never met the original DF did you, and I only met her when I was quite young and easily awed by her. She can still be awesome though of course I find her a lot more companionable now. I'm sure once you struck up an acquaintance with her you'd find her amenable…

Anyway if you're likely to be coming this way we shall always be glad to see you, though I'd advise you not to wait too long. Don't worry about feeling a waif after Death, there'll be Somebody there to collect you when we wander away in search of somewhere to go – at least I sincerely hope so.

  Blessings and KQ…

Bill

The Garden Office   12th April 2023

Hello Bill,
We had a pleasant trip to the stone circle at Stanton Drew yesterday. Our first proper explore in many months, given my need to recuperate and the bad weather we've had. In a sense I took you with us. Not that you were there in any kind of psychic sense, or that your *ka* was wandering among the stones. It was because of the book you wrote that you totally disliked and regretted: *The Rollright Ritual*. You told me it was your worst book, yet in some ways *I* feel it was your best. That's because you showed yourself as a *real* magician. For me, that's nothing to do with the plonking ritual itself, but because you described what you saw with your clairvoyance, and described your contacts with the souls who were long since gone and yet omnipresent. Call me old-fashioned but I do like to think that *real* magicians have Power rather than just verbosity, and you certainly had the former, as many will attest. You revealed yourself within the *Rollright Ritual* as you almost never did in your other books. Christine Hartley read this and opined: *He needs a good editor.* I knew from my own contacts with Weisers and Llewellyn that their editors were all a bit afraid of crossing you because they knew you were the Real Thing - who had no desire to ride a silver broomstick and sell millions. And so they left your prose alone when it could have done with a *bit* of honing. You did tend to labour the point, as Christine said.

My battered dog-eared first edition of the Ritual is in our Upper Room where all our 'occult' books are kept out of sight so as not upset friends, traders and neighbours. I'm too tired today to heave my scrawny corpus up there and squinny into your little book, yet I remember many odd lines... The countryside calling in its 'secret speech'; the 'Moon Maiden' who you felt has been sullied by the boots of astronauts; the stillness, the aliveness, the living, glistening, inward singing that catches the heart like First Love.

You dismissed the book, yet here on my pc I can see very high praise indeed being given by modern Seekers. Your lonely bicycle ride has accumulated many unseen quantum passengers over the decades. In their snippeted quotes, some of your writing is almost lyrical. I use the term 'corpus' in homage to you. I remember how you described your 'not uncorpulent corpus' cycling in the middle of night all the way from

'Nam to the Rollrights. That's about 30 miles over the hills, Bill! Christ, you had dedication - and you had balls. And I remember you writing that the one thing needed to make a connection with the lost energies and the forgotten souls of past and future who serve the those Stones is Love.

I've used that ever since, when visiting sites. My simplest invocation, following a respectful touch, goes something like: *The people who made these Stones once knew Love... and so do I.* Is that mawkish? Of course it's not these actual words as such but the feelings that need to be evoked, even if it means reaching into dark and painful places. Is that what method actors do?

Over the decades, this seems to have been as effective in its slow, old, often unseen way as any chanting, drumming or Words of Power could have been. Though I have also done a *lot* of Work with the Vowels and their Elements and Directions, as I also learned from you. Looking back, whenever I visit any ancient site there's a part of you being remembered. So among many other things I thank you for *all* this Bill.

Hmmm... a lot of very odd things happened after our simple visit to Stanton Drew but that's another story.

As for Carr Collins and DF getting disillusioned at the end of their lives... Regardie wrote great books on Magick, but I don't think he was a great magician. But I think he was right, in a sense. The great ceremonies and rituals of the Golden Dawn *were* amateur theatricals. How could they be otherwise? I've done enough Am-Dram in my time, and my performance of Bacchus at the U.Ky. is probably still talked about in hushed tones. When I see films of rituals I have to look through laced fingers and squirm. Yet I know that inwardly, for *some* of the participants, Cosmic Swirlings can be going on. My dearest friend, the late Mary Jack, once saw Laurence Oliver doing his lauded, crook-back Richard III at the Old Vic and was overwhelmed by the waves of the sexuality he projected. Yet when we (much later) watched the professional movie made of that same performance (to preserve his thespian magick for posterity), he just looked ridiculous. A Ham of Hams. 'It wasn't like that in person, Alan...'

So I think your comments about Laura Jennings fit in here too. She brought all her group to the UK to do public performances of the GD rites on some stage in London. Both Crowley and DF had done similar, so it's not as if she was after a quick buck (though she might have been!). When I gave a talk about the Horned God/dess in her place in Seattle in 94ish, she got her whole group to do a formal Banishing of the room afterward. I noted they used the old-fashioned Lesser Banishing Ritual of the Pentagram and were highly orchestrated. I later explained to them about your version, using the IAO and the Time/Space/Event lines of the Ring-Pass-Not but they weren't ready for that.

I note that on the 12th April 1988 you're talking about Gwyn ap Nudd, the Horned God of various names who, with his consort, became a dominant energy within my life in those years. It's 12th April 2023 today so we're in tune. I must look out toward the exploding lushness of trees and shrubs in our long and narrow garden and say hello to Them. Bobbie told me apropos of nothing: *Herne gives, but he also takes away.* I suppose I could write about large parts of my life as being pitched around that single revelation.

Ancestral memories… They're becoming increasingly important to me, as I get closer to joining them. If you're a resident of Wiltshire you can apply for a free Library Card, which to me is far more important than an American Express or any Platinum Level credit cards. It also means that I can, in the Library itself next to the Atrium, get free access to the *Ancestry* website. In short, I've since learned that on my mother's side I'm Irish! My lot seem to have come over to Scotland first, from Cavan, perhaps escaping the Great Famine, and then down to Newcastle. It feels right. I've always been struck how the Venerable Bede writing in the 8th Century described the peoples north of the Tyne as being Irish; and I once hitch-hiked around Eire trying to track down a notional past life near Lisdoonvarna. Yet it's not mere blood-lines that enthral me but Place, and the Land, and the Spirit of the Land and the Spirit of Place and how we traverse these realms. I have to go to Cavan now, even if it's only via Google Earth.

Hmmmmm….

Alan

Wm. G. Gray
14. Bennington St.
Cheltenham
Glos. GL50 4ED

Telephone

(0242) 24129

12SEP 1989

Alan,

As you'll see from enclosed script, Jacobus is in a hu-ha position with his Temple, even though everyone seems to be supporting him, and he's got some rich people in his group. So I've got <u>faint</u> hopes in his direction, though none at all with Mike Jamieson whom I don't believe has done one damn thing in <u>any</u> direction despite taking all my gear. I seriously doubt if he has <u>one</u> follower unless its someone useless and non-compos. But what else was there to do at the time? He was the one and only person with the slightest interest in the Sangreal Concept in the UK...All he has ever done is to moan about his ex and the rotten way she's treating him and the money she's extracting from him etc etc...I may be wronging him and indeed I <u>hope</u> so, but I don't have any real faith in nor hopes of Mike Jamieson….

I know about Marcia, and I think she's better this time for having had a couple of kids of her own which she's perfectly firm with, although absolutely fair and is doing a very good job of bringing them up. I don't think there's much doubt of her being DF, as you'll see if you ever meet her, which I hope you will some day, and she <u>can</u> still be difficult to deal with if she wants to be, though we don't really disagree about anything except I still won't accept blacks and she will, though I know she's doesn't have any in her group – or at least not yet anyway...

I'm in close contact with an old friend of Roy [Bowers] who has also done a book which Hales have taken if Doreen Valiente co-authors it, which she is doing at intervals. Of course her name is known and his isn't, simply being John Jones which is not exactly inspiring by itself…

"The Old Sod" IS an odd expression for Americans to appreciate as they don't 'get' a lot of our familiar sayings...So a sod is only a lump of earth to them.

Marcia doesn't get a hell of a lot of time for writing though she gets up very late in the morning, 10.30-11 sometimes. Marty gets his own breakfast and the kids away to school or day camp. Of course she does a lot of the "Psychic Fairs" and accepts a limited number of private clients for "psychic counselling" whatever that means. Apparently it's only legal in the State of New York if it's done as an act of entertainment. Exactly the same position that my own mother was in years ago. So naturally Marcia gets herself a certificate from some phoney Church, and on the strength of that otherwise valueless piece of paper can claim that what she's doing is "spiritual counselling" for which of course she can charge what she likes. In other words she's doing plain old-fashioned fortune telling under a lot of modern disguises, but thereby helping to keep her home going from a very necessary point of view.

Incidently, the thing that started in America about Roy Bowers without his knowledge and after his death purely from a few letters he'd written, is changing tactic lately. The "Head" of this "Roebuck" affair is now thinking of turning it into a "Church" purely for legal reasons. Ann Finnan, I remember her quite well and how thrilled they were to find I'd known Roy personally and still had a lot of his letters left, which they duly copied. I gather Doreen Valiente had a very soft spot for Roy with whom she had a brief extra-marital affair a number of years back under what we thought was comic circumstances. I also gather she's done a whole chapter about him in her latest book…

I like Laura Jennings personally, but not her payment policies, or for that matter the Golden dawn "teachings" which are outdated and over theatrical, and I can't think of any reason why she should like my letters which I only write just to be polite. For instance, Llewellyns sent me a magical script recently for "cover comments" which I couldn't very well give since it contradicted about all I'd ever done, and included Raphael as the Solar Archangel instead of Michael. So far as I known only Dion Fortune ever did this, and I'm convinced that Raphael has always been connected with the principle of healing, and what she didn't know was that this was only in relation to hurts and wounds or traumas, whether spiritual or physical. So far as organic or inherited disease is concerned, the Solar Archangel Michael is the acceptable Judaeo-Christian substitute for Apollo the God Healing. Dion made a number of mistakes in her Mystical Qabalah due to her lack of Hebraic knowledge specifically, and I'm sure this one was because of her own need of healing which she was quite aware of on <u>sub</u>conscious levels yet could not face on surface ones...I feel sure her troubles in life were sexual, and her refusal to accept the perfectly natural and normal needs of human beings in that direction. That's not a mistake she's likely to make again.

Bobbie of course sends her best regards to you, but would be interested to know how she came to inspire you with an inclination to write about the Horned God whom she only see in the purely Celtic Cernunnos light. Or possibly Herne. But she does remember telling you of her conviction concerning Camelot, which I can't honestly say I share with her. Don't leave it too long before you plan that picnic.

Glad to have heard from you while I still have a chance. Now I'd better get this in the slot if I can stagger that far.

Bill

THE OLD SOD

The Atrium   13th April I think

Hello Bill,
Storm Noa is in full blast here as the Atrium roof is being pounded by hail and 75 mph wind. Lightnings and thunders in the sky above. Is this what they call Thundersnow? I've never heard anything like it, and I love it. Youngsters are flocking to the door to take photos, but I'll bet the U3A will be plodding boldly onward to show the 'snowflakes' with their iPhones the true power of the Oldie.

Oh, Mike Jamieson… I've actually trimmed down your comments and will tell you now that I'm on *his* side. As far as anyone could tell, you and Bobbie had a reasonably happy marriage. When you 'banished' me in 1974 I was going through my own sorts of hell through my job (at which I made a complete cock-up), and the failure of my relationship at that time with Laura. She actually contacted me via Facebook a few years ago and apologised, and said she made the wrong choice of fella, but I don't do forgiveness easily – if at all. Bill, you had no understanding of the pain, despair and bewilderment that Mike Jamieson was clearly going through. To you it made no sense: how could anything distract from the Sangreal? How dare he! As for myself, I was just a young eejit who never wanted to join your group and for whom 'Magic' was little more than a nine-month wonder. So I'm on Mike's side in all this and if you meet on the Other Side *you* should apologise. Other than the death of a child, there is no pain worse than what he went through, nothing more bewildering. Until *that* aspect of the Heart gets sorted, then all else on every level is secondary.

I actually saw some of the clunky stuff you passed on to him but there was no inherent *mana* in it. I'd have been polite and taken it and dumped it after doing some terse ritual to make amends. I *was* jealous of you giving Bob Stewart your crystal, though. And of course that makes me think of what and who I should pass my own stuff on to after I'm gone. Hmmm…

Marcia… I'm just wondering if I've created a False Memory of having met her. I think I must have. We certainly corresponded, and I never had any sense of the fierceness you warned me about. Her letters were cheery and kind. She also attempted some distant healing on me and although it didn't work, the effort alone was important. And I know that she *did* accept Blacks without telling you. In fact you had many good phone conversations with a couple of them who knew of your racism, but didn't want to throw out the baby with the bath-water, so to speak. You had no idea. Is that what later caused your (I was told) explosive break-up?

Evan John Jones... I had numerous chats with him, and I persuaded Carl W. of Llewellyn to publish a book he'd written. I think it had something to do with Masks in Ritual. Or maybe something else. I won't google this one. He was a working-class lad who certainly knew his stuff and explained it clearly. And he really enjoyed using the term 'Witch', though he probably didn't tell you that in case you got your Etymological Dictionary out. I'm not mocking that last. One of my most important books gives the etymological origins of Wiltshire place-names. It has been a gold mine of revelations for my own Work.

DF's 'sexual needs'... I believe you're right. Plus I'm certain she had a deep, dark secret that she did her best to conceal at the time, that wouldn't cause the slightest eye-lid batting today. As I said earlier, I believe that she was epileptic. The bodily convulsions she described in *Psychic Self Defence* were not caused by psychic attacks, but because she was having a *grand mal*. And these were caused by masturbation. Or so the specialists assured everyone. Even in my day, this was defined in the standard dictionaries as 'self abuse' and 'bodily self-pollution'!

Yes, her generation was that backward. When Crowley boasted he had 'sacrificed babies' many times, the reason he wasn't arrested was because the cognoscenti knew that this was a slang term for wanking. So they smiled and left him alone and probably tossed themselves silly at the very thought. I think that my generation was the first to escape from that sort of nonsense. I think that Crowley played no small part in setting us free.

Bobbie felt that Camelot was near Almondsbury. I never did get to take her there, did I? The real Camelot was in South /wales, as detailed by the marvellous books of Wilson and Blackett that I've only recently discovered.

The storm, the storm... Should I invoke the Chinese Weather Magician within me to fend off the torrential rain? I'll have a go.

alan

Wm. G. Gray
14. Bennington St.
Cheltenham
Glos. GL50 4ED

Telephone

(0242) 24129

19 SEPT 1989

Dear Alan, well thanks for your letter with your explanation in it, though I still don't think much of being called an Old Sod, but if you're set on it you will obviously do it regardless of whether I'm alive or dead. That little detail won't matter a sod to you one way or another. Still you might have called me the Old Shithouse or the Terrible Turd, or something equally nasty like Shitface, or just to be smart Excrement Expression or Poopwhistle or something quite ridiculous, However, I would like you to make it clear that this was your idea and nobody else's (unless of course everybody else has being calling me something nasty behind my back for years and I've never got to know about it till now).

    I know Robert Turner called me about every name he could think of the other year at Carr's ridiculous Guildhall "do". If I remember he was screaming in the end and all I could do was to laugh helplessly because he looked so childish and absurd hopping from foot to foot and mouthing obscenities that only sounded ridiculous. He was screeching: "You bastard, you bastard, I hate you and all I want to do is piss on your grave. You know fuck-all about anything you ignorant shit. You wouldn't even know the right way to pick a book on magic up, you shit, you turd. I hate you do you hear me?? I <u>HATE YOU</u>! You've insulted my wife. I demand an apology at once AT ONCE!" (Here I pointed out that I wouldn't even know his wife as such) Meantime he was attracting so much attention to himself that people were beginning to remonstrate while I was pointing out the futility of pissing on a non-existent grave and even old Carr was bothering a bit. In fact the only one unworried and no more than mildly concerned was <u>me</u>. I still haven't a clue who his wife was, or even for that matter, that he <u>was</u> married. I felt like asking to see her out of sheer curiosity just to view what sort of a woman who would marry a piece of crap like him. So after having being very thoroughly insulted by Robert Turner, I don't feel anyone is likely to do better. Strange to say no fewer than two people present in that room died since. Poor old Carr, and Colin Murray killed himself with Yew, just as Roy Bowers did except a different poison.

You're possibly right about Mike Jamieson, except that its so depressing. And so far as I know, all he's done is to lose someone's address which might have been useful. I had a letter today from New York which shows how some of the Yanks are getting on with it, but of course they're shortening the Sangreal Sacrament. They must shorten and condense everything or it wouldn't be them.

Incidentally, I had what I thought <u>might</u> be an interesting idea, and got Marcia to send me her horoscope, hoping I might find something between that and the Dion Fortune Noon Map in Carr's book, but there wasn't a <u>thing.</u> Or at least not at first glance. Though I don't think there's very much doubt about her identity. Her husband Marty says we're a couple of awkward sods who deserve each other. I like Marty. Ironically <u>this</u> time she's practising as a psychic consultant, and there she (DF) was forbidding everybody to practice it last time. I'm pretty sure it was sex that jiggered DF up last time. Why those two unkept appointments with a <u>Freudian</u> psychiatrist??? At least she doesn't have those absurd hang-ups any longer, but a lot of women did in those days. Sex was still a taboo subject in her time, even though there was a hell of a lot more freedom. There are still "things you didn't talk about" believe this or not.

And yet, the old Hebrews treated it with considerable reverence if not awe. They might as well have named their God F*U*C*K, because with the final and the dagesh in, the IHVH Name, was written so:

יהוה

[hand-written in original letter]

Thus the Yod was a speck of sperm, the first Heh an empty cervix, the Vav an erect phallus, and the final Heh a filled cervix, That was the way they saw it, because the whole word stood for the sex-act, which was why they revered it so much and were so careful with it, There are lots of similar symbols and "hidden meanings" under comparative phraseologies. For example the well known "Om mani padme hum" literally means "Oh the Jewel in the Lotus", but euphemistically it means Oh the Penis in the Vagina. And of course the Spear in the Cup to designate the Grail is almost too obvious. So is the Rose and the Cross. Or for that matter any suitable or even possible combination of artefacts, So long as you could visualise male and female coupling somehow, That was all it needed.

Oddly enough (or is it really?) a little while back a lot of the clergy were complaining about their "Yoo Hoo" prayerbooks since they were translated from the Latin "Deus qui ex etc etc" as "God, you who are etc etc", whereas in fact the sonics Yoo Hoo Arr (or IEU Hu AR) were almost the same as IHV or possibly the chanty Yo Ho Heave Ho. Slight variation, that's all….

Incidentally I've solved the question why Roy Bowers chose the name Tubal Caine. He simply got it out the White Goddess as a smith-god because it happened to be there. Had it been Vulcan or Haephestus it might have been them instead.

I don't know there is any wonder or atmosphere behind my life. OK, so I'm an Old Sod, on old Bastard, a thousand different kinds of shit if you like, but I am a human being who loved the esoteric Tradition I tried to serve, and which both Jacobus and Marcia were part of too. Perhaps I didn't do very well with what I've got, but I did my best with it all, and anybody who doesn't like it can stuff it all up with the aid of a garden shovel and a pitchfork or two, then roll it all flat with with one of the Mills of God which can be thrown away afterwards. Or something like that anyway.

So that's it for the time being. The next couple of weeks will be a bit sticky for Bobbie so I hope everything goes OK. Please keep all your fingers crossed. My regards to your wife and family. God alone knows what they've heard about me if anything, but please make it clear that you must allow for imagination.

                          Blessings and KQ.

Bill

In our Sitting Room   15th April 2023

I'm working on my laptop, keeping an eye out for Dave the Builder coming, to sort out some problems in our lovely little house. It's an old, two bedroom Victorian semi that was built for the railway workers when the network was exploding. Parts of it, like me, need some attention.

Touched a nerve, judging from your last letter. Nobody called you an old sod or anything else behind your back, as far as I'm aware. Then again, I met very few people to even discuss you. I chose the title myself, and take full responsibility. Jacobus hated it. Thousands of his Sangreal Sodality members were up in arms, he said.

Am a bit run down today, but I don't want to become one of those old men who spend all their time talking about their ailments. I *am* a bit worried about my heart and have also been peeing blood. I'm wondering whether I'll be Called Away when this book is finished, as I can't imagine I'll ever write another. Yet there are places I want to visit and things I want to do before then, and I don't think Margaret will cope without me – or even want to cope.

Your piece about YHVH is brilliant. I've written a couple of books on the kabbalah but I still can't recognise a single Hebrew letter – and nor do I need to or want to. I've always known that I'm a second-rate intellectual and a third-rate academic who has used style to hide the fact that I often haven't a clue. Have I said that before? It's not me being falsely modest: it's a forensic analysis of my own phoneyness.

Oh – I think it was actually a *Jungian* psychologist she had an appointment with. I used to know his name.

I'm very tired. I must go crash…

                Best

                Alan

Wm. G. Gray
14. Bennington St.
Cheltenham
Glos. GL50 4ED

Telephone

(0242) 24129

22 SEP 1989

Dear Alan,

Thanks for yours undated but here today the 22nd, Don't believe a word about Roy Bowers. As I think I made it plain in my script, the only one I ever heard of him "initiating" was Ann Slowgrove, who rang me up later to say she'd kept her fingers crossed the whole time so none of it counted, and then later Roy rang to tell me he didn't trust her, so had put on a totally fake ceremony which didn't amount to anything anyway so it didn't count. Roy did invite me to a couple of his "dos", but quite a number of other people were there too, including Gerard Noel and of course the ubiquitous Dezzie Burke. That man belonged to more occult things than you could shake a stick at. Apart from being the Sec of the SRIA, and a Mason of Templar Grade, plus the 2nd IC Druid and probably long since the Pendragon, he was a Sar of the Holy Syrian Church and God alone knows what else.

I only know that when Roy "initiated" old Doreen, she was about ten seconds "claiming her rights" and dragging him off to bed while others kept wary watch for her husband, dear little soul. That was one thing Roy didn't really want to do, but was hoist with his own petard so to speak, because he'd invented that local rule himself, namely that if a male asked a female in his group for sex, she would be entitled to refuse him, but NOT if it were the other way around, be cause that would amount to "rejecting the Goddess", so he would have to do the best he could. I'm told it was a hasty affair. Having invented the rule for his own convenience with somebody else, Roy got jammed with it for his <u>in</u>convenience with Doreen who I gather was a very demanding and insistent partner. Serve the bugger right! I notice Ann Slowgrove didn't haul him off to bed pronto. But then you must remember that poor old Doreen had then had a lot of her guts hauled out and her hormones were all playing bloody hell.

So make it quite clear that I have no, Repeat NO, repeat again <u>NONE WHATSOEVER</u> connection with any form of "Witchcraft", and in the words of Jacobus Swart, wouldn't even piss on them if they were on fire. I am all _for_ human beings both male and female worshipping a Feminine Aspect of Deity, and in fact have just recently brought out a book on that very topic, BUT, the second they start calling themselves "Witches", that's when I blow up and explode. At the same time I wouldn't give a shit if they'd call it differently, or call it anything else whatsoever. Pagans or whatever.

Yes, I liked Roy as a human being and fellow creature, though I disagreed with a lot of what he claimed, and certainly couldn't take him very seriously, except that he _did_ carry out that healing ceremony when he said he would, and it _did_ work. But that was a natural ability, and had nothing to do with "witchcraft" whatever he said. I'm still very good friends with John Jones at Brighton and we write fairly frequently. And John is even bringing a book out with old Doreen. I felt and still feel genuinely sorry about Roy, because I thought it such a waste of a life for nothing worth bothering about. A hell of a lot of so-called Ancient Tradition was nothing but pure bullshit. The now much talked about 1734 plate as a family heirloom for instance. Absolute balls. Doreen got it for £5 in the Lanes where she bought most of her junk. He also used the name "Robert Cochrane" purely as a pen-name to prevent people connecting him with "Witch" activities, since he worked for a firm which produced type design for Churches, and they had some Moslem clients too. So he _was_ justified there.

The only thing that Roy ever "taught" me in any sense, was an explanation of his spiritual system as such, and it was _as this_ that I copied it out and published what I had _from that source_. And yes, he _did_ seem to hang around quite a while after he died, and we had a bit of a job getting rid of him. Incidentally, he filled up old Justine Glass's head full of crap _on purpose_ just because she was doing a book about "witchcraft" at the time. Same as Sandra's friends got Halloween hats and put on a totally fake "Witchcraft Gathering" for the benefit of Hans Holzer the American journalist who lapped it all up like cream and whined for more. I question how many other "do"s have been equally phoney, and written purely for the sake of sensational reading. Probably more than either of us could guess. As for Roy having initiated "many now national figures in British Occultism", I'll quote that to John next week and you'll probably hear the howl from Brighton. Neither of us had heard that shit before, and I'd like whoever wrote it to stand up in court and substantiate it. And for the record, the only people I've ever initiated are those concerned with the Sangreal Concept - except Mike Jamieson, It wasn't that I didn't like or even trust the man, because I do personally. It's just that I don't have any beliefs or reliance in him whatsoever. Which may sound a hell of a pity, but there it is.

Incidentally and while I think of it, Bobby tells me that Roy had a healthy respect or her, This could have been because she saw through his pretences or never seemed in the slightest impressed with him. Quite probably a combination of both factors….

OK we'll keep that [*after-death Code Word*] private.

Incidentally, did you know there is a huge cavern under the Tor? It's full of vast tanks of water.

I hadn't realised you'd had all that hassle with "communicators" ref DF. If you get any bright boys and girls sending messages of "sweetness and light" from me, tell em to go and do something rude with themselves. I'm far more likely to send a vast great razzberry instead, or tell a dirty story. Now the one way you'd know it couldn't possibly be me, is if I ever seemed to turn against or seriously disparage my own race.

I got Marcia's map yesterday, and was vaguely hoping there might be come comparison with Dion Fortune's Solar Chart, but there just isn't a thing to compare, Still it's interesting. As far as I'm concerned I'm happy with her company on this earth, and so far as I know both she and her husband Marty are happy with mine. Its like Jacobus and Gloria. To me, they're family. In fact it's this country where I feel so lost and unwanted apart from Bobbie. Keep your fingers crossed when she goes in next Thursday for the op. (Keep them crossed for me also that I don't fall over my feet, down the stairs or any other damn silly trick.)

Thanks a lot and KQ,

Bill

Garden Office   16th April 2023

Dear Bill,

The rain is coming down again, but not torrential. The birds are back, attacking the seeds and mealworms; and all sorts of people who were/are connected with you are flocking in via Social Media, doing similar: Doreen, the Crowthers, Dusty Miller, Ann Finnan, Lord Eldon, Thomas More, Wheatley, the SIL, Regardie, Basil Wilby... Sometimes I think if I sit in any one place long enough, the entire Universe will express itself. That's the message I got from the tarot card known as *The Chariot*, that you so brilliantly analysed in the Talking Tree.

Oh and I've just seen the evil cat sneak past the door.. You liked cats didn't you? So do I, but I wouldn't have one. When yours jumped on my knee at my first visit, you went *Crikey!* or something like that, as it never did that to anyone. I think I passed some kind of test there and then.

Yes, I knew about the caves under the Tor and the huge water tanks. I think every Sacred Hill is said to be hollow, or with caves. My own favourite, on which I want my ashes scattered, is Cley Hill. The legend there is of a Golden Ram within a hidden cave. I suppose that's something to do with the Templars who owned portions of the adjoining land. On the other hand, if there's any credence in the reports of those who have seen UFO's dissolving into the hill, it must be stacked with space-craft from distant Galaxies, like some cosmic breaker's yard. I often visualise myself on the adjoining Little Cley Hill, on which I've done a lot of solo magick, and try to 'enter' the larger mass. And/or make inner contact with Bugley, the King of Faery said to reside there.

The code-word... of course I remember it. In the years since I've had sessions with many exceptional mediums. Some of them have given me evidential messages that I deeply needed, though I often didn't realise this until later. To me, this is far more important than the channelled stuff from Ascended Masters who never say anything new or surprising. Yet I've not had the slightest peep from you. Perhaps you're in your place of Perfect Peace Profound. I hope so. I dimly recall some bizarre story (probably from Jacobus), that whoever accepted your Wand/Rod would also have to take on your remaining karma. That sounds like the sort of offer you'd get from a used-car dealer. I'd never have accepted it.

Or maybe I'm just creating another False Memory in the urge to spin a good yarn.

I wasn't hassled with DF's 'communicators' so much as nudged. I remember you and I had various discussions about 'Lord Eldon' who was the powerful Inner Contact behind Christine Hartley and Kim Seymour. And lo! Even as I type this, someone has just popped up on Facebook who has just been Eldon's old place in County Durham. She mentioned the name co-incidentally, without any sense of his link with the Stella Matutina and indeed the SIL. Whoever or whatever Eldon is, or was, or will be, I do seem to have had energies and impulses from him over the years.

Oh – did my act of 'Assuming the God Form' of the Chinese Weather Magician fend off the storm as I walked home a couple of days ago? Yes. Storm Noa held off for me and I walked home in sunshine, then it all exploded again. I have my moments, Bill.

As for Roy Bowers aka Robert Cochrane... I like reading about him as a Rascal Guru, but if I'd met him when I was young I'd probably have been completely taken in. I didn't have Bobbie's no-nonsense insight. Yet in retrospect I see that my own Inners – whatever They are – protected me in odd ways. I'd meet decent, brilliant magically-inclined people who were perfectly nice to me, yet I often got a powerful and inexplicable impulse to Keep Away from them. Decades later, I'm glad I did.

I've just had a peek at 'tomorrows' letter from you. I do remember parts of this, as Marcus and I made good use of it in *The Old Sod*. It's about your near-death experience as a lad when you were transported either onto another world or into another dimension. It was truly extraordinary; exactly what I would have expected and wanted from you...

Wm. G. Gray
14. Bennington St.
Cheltenham
Glos. GL50 4ED

Telephone

(0242) 24129

4 NOV 1989

Dear Alan, Well I'll do the best I can to remember what I can although it was a good many year ago since my last memory, yet that is so vivid it remains with me deeply if not completely clearly to this day. It wasn't so much the place, (which could have been almost anywhere) as the people who could only have been ones own in every possible sense of the word. There was just no such thing as a stranger. ALL were intimately related, and somehow they knew everything there might be to know about you, and you did the same for them. Somehow you were each other. It was the most wonderful and incredible feeling of expanded identity that could be imagined, Yet there were separate families and dwelling places etc which were somewhat strange from our point of view, since they had so little in them that we would recognise as "possessions" or "furniture" in the ordinary sense. What you wanted you made with your mind, but most people seemed to want so little except to be happy and comfortable. I remember one event was at a Temple where there was some kind of a ceremony going on at which there were acolytes wearing red cassocks with bunches of white cords at the shoulders, and at one point they all leaped in to the air clapped their hands above their heads and laughed heartily. I was deeply shocked, but a man with a short beard wearing sort of overalls standing next to me, put a kindly hand-on my shoulder and murmured in my ear: "Don't you know that laughter is one of the highest forms of worship?" I did NOT know that at the time, though I have learned this since.

 Then there was the library which was the most gigantic place I have ever seen, with one floor above another indefinitely. I could not see my guide's face, but knew he was wearing reddish robes. He told me they had every book ever written on earth, and I enquired anxiously: "Oh do you have Magick by the Master Therion?" having just seen the advertisement for Crowley's book in the "Occult Review", while not knowing who had written it. My guide sounded amused and replied: "Yes, we even have that" and whizzing me to another floor bent down and took a book from a low shelf, showed it to me and tossed it on the floor again. I bent to retrieve it, but he prevented me gently saying it was worthless, it would find its way back again.

Once there came a moment when I realised I was being initiated into something and sent back to my body to make a brief contact then return for the remainder of the ceremony. I woke up, sat briefly upright in bed and murmured "I will remember" than sank back to sleep forthwith. I, do not remember what happened then.

The sad time came when I knew there would be no more meetings with my "family" for the rest of my mortal life, because I must get on with what I had to do and be, none of which would be very notable yet was there for me to accomplish somehow. It was all part of "The Work" whatever that might be. I wasn't going to get much good from it myself, but I would always be welcome home when my time was done. The sense of separation was acute, and do you know I can still feel it? Both Marcus and Marcia are fellow-citizens of wherever that might have been.

In a vague way the "houses" seemed to be domed, and the "power" was in the dome, finding its way there from the "sun". I sort of remember someone talking; about it and saying: "Look, I could do this if I wanted to," and a heavy candlestick left the mantelpiece(?) by itself, wandered away a few feet then went back again, after which he explained that you had to learn how to live without interfering with other peoples arrangements of their belongings, otherwise life became impossible, Oh there seemed to be definite laws governing the interrelationship of everything in that state of existence. It was just a matter of knowing and observing them.

But as for saying that I encountered this that or the other person, or defining any specific soul individually as whoever - no I couldn't possibly, because I just don't have a clue. Nobody to my knowledge announced they were any particular person, and I wouldn't have believed them if they had. What cut me up was the knowledge that I hadn't yet achieved a sufficient state of "goodness" (for want of a better term) to stay with those people on a more permanent basis.

Yet they weren't what I would call "Superpeople" from any outstanding viewpoint. I mean they looked and behaved much as we do in many ways. But they just didn't have the capability of practising real evil. They seemed to have evolved past that point altogether, if you see what mean. Incidentally I don't remember any motor vehicles or anything really noisy or in the least violent. Nor did there seem to be anything like football crowds or discos, yet everyone was <u>intensely</u> happy and glowing with health. I have no idea of their social structure, but they were obviously more than contented with what they'd got. Somehow they seemed to do everything with their <u>minds</u> and know exactly what they ought to do. Yet they had theaters and places of entertainment, but I don't remember any form of currency. Oh yes, I can just remember one remark that was made there which impressed me and I've just remembered. A man was speaking, and he said (these are the exact words) "I can't tell you how wonderful it is not to have to be one person any longer. Why do you know, within reason, I can be almost anybody I like." The "within reason" was heavily accented. Don't ask me what was meant by that, I've no idea.

    Now for me to say Marcia is Dion Fortune back again is terribly simplistic and I suppose you could argue on the ins and outs of it for ever, but as far as <u>I'm</u> concerned its the same soul or rather identity, though certainly not the same <u>person</u> because your personality dies when you do, or should do anyway. Mind you she'd developed her persona so strongly, that it would survive a good deal of death.

    Anyhow she likes the idea of doing a book about "Earthing" and says she will push on with it because it hasn't been done at all that I know of, except that she touched on it very lightly in "Psychic Self Defence" but hasn't gone into it at all deeply. Actually the topic has been realised since time immemorial, yet not been examined in depth and exactly analysed as a psychological structure.

    I know that when people read biographies what fascinates them is not so much the person's character or accomplishments as their peculiarities and odd customs, because readers can relate with those one way or the other, especially whatever diminishes whoever it may be. For example Alfred letting cakes burn, or Bruce watching a spider or Gerald Gardner being bonded and beaten. It's the trivialities that count, so you're looking for things like that with me. Well I haven't done anything great or famous apart from writing a few somewhat original esoteric books which are only of interest in their own very limited field. I can't claim to have been anybody famous in a previous incarnation or to have been controlled or even overshadowed by some wonderful Spirit Guide (Ycch!). I've done my best to give you a genuine story or two, but what people are going to say is: "If he was all that good, why did he finish up so arthritic and useless?" OK, so why did Crowley finish up a registered drug-addict? Or Dion Fortune die of leukaemia? Or for that matter why was Jesus crucified as a political prisoner? There were thousands crucified along the Appian Way after the Spartacus rebellion, why did not any of them get famed for anything? In fact I suppose you could just ask one big WHY? and leave it at that. Isn't that what Life is all about? How long has humanity been asking that question????

At the present time my leg ulcers are back, so I've got the District Nurse coming in to dress it for me twice a week. While I think of it, don't bother with a Christmas Card for me, I'm cutting mine to almost none this year, otherwise its going to cost a fortune in stamps and I don't love the Post Office all that much. I never cared for Christmas cards anyway, people who can't bother to drop you a line for a whole year send you hypocritical printed good wishes at that one time and think they've done a social duty. Bah, humbug. (Yes, why don't they have cards with Bah, Humbug, Long live Scrooge. on them?)

     Hope all this helps. Bill.

Garden Office   Monday, I think.

Hello Bill,

I've just heard that Dusty Miller has died. Aged 88. Although you dissed the products on his stall, I swear by them. And the man himself. He was different, deliciously so. In fact he even asked me to write his biography when I visited him at his home in Strood, saying I could keep all the royalties. I'd have loved to, but had to explain that I'm not a full-time writer and sales of my books are dismal, and so I just couldn't afford to do this. He did eventually get one launched, and I was first to buy it. I've told the two wands he gave me about his death, but I'm sure they already knew. We'll light a candle for him tonight.

Your vision/transportation...

'Somehow you *were* each other...' I do think that's crucial to all life everywhere. You would know yourself of the Gnostic belief that life and the Universe can be summed as All is One. I think this is something that you either 'get', deep in your bones or merely acknowledge as a simplistic piece of philosophy.

I am you, Bill. You are me. Though I don't think you were ever central to my own 'inner tribe', and was perhaps more of an awkward overlap from yours. Think of of me more as an Amenable Neighbour who will never get too close to your property, and just pop my head over the fence to say G*ood morning Bill!*

Still a bit low today, as I still get a bit frightened. Over the past months I've had moments when I've feared that another heart-attack might be coming; I've wondered whether I should use my GTN spray and call an ambulance. Instead I sit quietly in some café, or in the library, and wait for it to pass. Which it has done, obviously. How much of this is just normal tiredness from my therapeutic brisk walking? I haven't told Margaret as she is a terrible worrier. In fact she had it worse than me when they helicoptered from the Isle of Wight to Southampton: she was stuck on the island not knowing if I was still alive, dreading the phone call.

And so I worry that when this MS is finished, They will decide that my own Work is done and my Dad will appear to take me across.

But please Bill, much as I sort of loved you in my own cold, distant way, I don't want *you* there offering to do so. You knew nowt about football, and that to me always counted against you.

Now I've just peeked into the folder containing the Second Tranche: there's only a couple of letters left. So we're both coming to some sort of an end, symbolically or literally...

alan

14 Bennington St
CHELTENHAM
Glos GL50 4ED
31 DEC 1989

Dear Alan

So far as I'm concerned Mike Jamieson is persona non grata and in my opinion is no longer fit to represent the Sangreal in this country or anywhere else... He has become so obsessed with personal hatred for his ex-mate...that he has written to Joe Terc, Warden of the Bronx Sangreal Sodality...requesting that his Temple work a Rite of Commination against this woman to whom he was never married in the first place...

As you probably know, a commination ceremony is the nearest thing we have to a curse, bit it is usually as "Judica me Deus et discerne causa meum de genta non sancta" sort of thing, which is an appeal for justice and a specification of the cause for it and whom or what it is against. But it is NOT as a rule for any type of personal vengeance or for spiteful reasons whatsoever.... Mike was NOT the person I would have chosen to represent the Sangreal in this country... and for that that I blame the Sangreal itself. Altogether I've only had about four people express the slightest interest, but as soon as they knew that might have to do something, I never heard another word...

I've had copies of my Swansong Book on the Goddess... Also Doreen sent us a copy of her latest which Bobbie is reading through at mealtimes and muttering "Balls" and other mild obscenities every so often. I rather liked it... I see it as being autobiographical to quite an extent. At the moment I'm cooperating with Marcia on a book to do with "Earthing", a surprisingly deep and involved subject of supreme spiritual significance....

13 JAN 1990

Dear Alan

Another moan for that bio. Before you say too many good things about Jacobus in South Africa, see if you or anyone can find out why he never bothers to answer my letters and simply ignores them all. When Weisers turned down my Bloodmother book he wanted to produce it, then messed around for over three years and produced - nothing. Weisers were turning down all my stuff now because old Carr's dollars weren't behind me any more, so I had to do <u>something.</u> I hastily re-wrote the thing plus a few extra bits, and Llewellyns grabbed it. It's on the market now and I've had my complimentaries. It was to have been called the Bloodmother, but instead Llewellyns called it Evoking the Primal Goddess. Anyhow I wrote out and told Jacobus who never bothered to answer for so long that I got fed up to the teeth and then wrote him an "Oh then go to hell" note. The very next day a letter came from him in which he wailed away about being a rotten correspondent <u>but</u> he hadn't really lied, was just economical with the truth and some friend had advised him not to send the letter he was going to, so that's why I hadn't had it. So naturally I write straight back saying bloody fool why ask someone else what to send, etc? Plus I'd fixed it so that he inherited Weisers books, while Marcia gets the Llewellyns ones. She'll probably be better off in the end since they're picking up all Weisers sling out...

Anyway, I've written 7 letters all of which have been ignored by Jacobus and we used to be very close friends. He swore he'd enclosed a letter to her in a letter she got after I was home after last time, and she swore there wasn't, but the packet had been torn so I don't know which one is lying but I shouldn't think it was Marcia.

At the moment we're doing a book together on "Earthing". I'm supplying material while she's doing the write-up and padding it out. There's some interesting bits in it here and there, and I've been careful to include some sex-bits too, otherwise you've a job to sell it these days. Now there was a faint chance that Jacobus might have got a bit jealous of Marcia though I wouldn't have thought it likely. I'm much too shaky to make it out there again. I've asked him over and over again <u>why</u> he just doesn't write but he just won't tell me anything. Just ignores everything.

Anyway, Laura Jennings wrote again sending a "Portal" with about everyone I don't like. Mostly Chaos Magic... I haven't a clue why they would bother with me. I don't have a lot of time for them and Chaos...

In any case, make it plain that this deliberate ignoring me like this has made the end of my life unhappy and has hurt me quite a lot. Fortunately Marcia hangs on.

    God bless and KQ

                    Bill

Garden Office   17th April

Hello Bill...

I severely edited and conjoined those last two letters, neither of which bore the Sangreal heading. I still remember absolutely NOTHING about them, as you might say in block capitals. I'm sure that I wouldn't have replied to either. I only enclose even these because they're examples of what seems to happen in every magic(k)al group. Think of all those esoteric acronyms: AA, GD, FIL, SIL, FOI, OTO, OCS, SOL, AMORC, to name but a few. Plus every witch coven you could possibly name, and also your own SS. Some members of every group have hissy fits with the leaders and become renegades and sometimes the whole thing splinters and explodes (like that damned Sangreal seems to have done). Perhaps, when they get enlightened or illuminated, they feel they can do better themselves and so kick up or just walk away, muttering. I suppose it happens in every sphere of life, not just anything occult.

Your letters made me sad though. And I don't want to utter those dread words *I told you so*. But I suppose I just have!

I'm glad I kept out of it all, and was never a joiner of anything much. I wasn't wise, so much as lucky. Though I am aware that I also missed out on a lot because of the delicious gossip.

Your words, in trying to make sense of the bad choice of Mike Jameison...'for that that I blame the Sangreal itself'. It must have painful for you to say that Bill, instead of thinking it was down to your own lack of insight.

Honestly, what did the Sangreal give you but an endless sense of tension and betrayal? Using the system from the SIL, did it give you: Power? Love? Wisdom? I've also stumbled on a very long and loving letter to me from Bobbie who goes into great and disturbing detail about your final months. You went through hell – and you put her through worse

What use *was* the Sangreal? Honestly? And I'm even sadder because you still have the highest hopes for Marcia, yet I know that you're soon to have an even worse falling out with her. I don't know why this happened/will happen, and although I have a delightful contact with Marty I don't even *want* to know and won't ask him.

And then there was a piece I found a piece that was misplaced at the very back of the Second Tranche, and so I'll give this now, and put the Sangreal Heading back on as a kind of forlorn hope…

Alan

Wm. G. Gray
14. Bennington St.
Cheltenham
Glos. GL50 4ED

Telephone

(0242) 24129

[Undated]

THE LAST GASP,

Suddenly my godson Marcus who visits me about once a week and had been reading some of my books, announced that he has met a most interesting nan who happened to be living only a couple of streets from me, and was very interested in esoteric topics. I naturally invited him to visit me and shortly discovered some very interesting facts. He was a very pleasant youngish and slightly bearded man of about thirty three or four, slim, but he also had had an Austrian Rosicrucian mentor, just as I had previously, though not from the same Order, but I believe they were connected. Anyway he had taught Kevin what was needed to know about the Western Inner Tradition and even initiated him with a traditional ceremony. This could not possibly have been coincidence by any chance. There could not have been the slightest doubt that I was witnessing an intentional intervention of the Sangreal Itself manifesting on the material plane of personalities.

On a scale of weekly visits I introduced Kevin to the Sangreal ideology in which he proclaimed himself vitally interested and fully prepared to back it up with the very best of his ability. After satisfying each other of our bona fides, I scraped together what Mike had left of the small Temple and formally initiated Kevin on the best day of the year - Vernal Equinox 1990. How we scraped through it I shall never quite be certain, by this time my walking had got so bad I was staggering and stumbling about all over the place and had to support myself on sticks most of the time, but one way or another it got done.

Kevin was now a duly initiated member of the Sangreal Sodality with responsibilities to fulfil towards other Companions. He was hoping to start a small Temple either in his own house or that of my godson whom he hoped to initiate himself maybe towards Midsummer...

There was one thing I was glad about. Kevin had a much more charismatic figure than I have, and he should be able to attract people I could never gain attention from in person however much my books might interest them. So I have faint hopes that he might possibly stir up some slight interest in the Sangreal Concept here in the UK before he is finished, and in any case I cant possibly do any more. I've just come to the end of my tether and there's nothing else left to do. I've got to the stage where if it goes it goes and if it doesn't it doesn't and I'm leaving it to itself to do whatever it pleases.

Bill

Garden Office.   Same day

Hello Bill,
I feel a bit more cheerful and optimistic today, and am chasing up various medical folks to get me sorted physically. M has just coming buzzing in to tell me about her own Inner Work that is far ahead of anything I've ever experienced. Her connections are with the group she belongs to on-line, small and largely American. I suppose that's the way all things are going on now. Perhaps the Sangreal – whatever it is – will only take off if someone does something Virtual. Is that the right term? I actually think that you in your prime, as a former member of the Signals Regiment in the Army., would have taken to this sort of thing very happily.

I see on the news, with respect to the forthcoming Coronation, people with placards bearing the words: 'Not My King'... I can understand that. I suspect that if anyone reads this book of ours they might be crying into the aethyrs: *Not **My** Sangreal!* when they see your own take on it.

I met Kevin at your funeral. You bigged him up in your letter more than I've included here. At the reception afterward, the acoustics of the room were very poor and I wasn't wearing my hearing aid and was keen to escape anyway, but Kevin sort of whispered to me about having been given your Sword and Book. The Book was sealed, and you had given him the injunction – no, the *command* – not to open it until well after his death. He also half-whispered some yarn about someone having died shortly after he had inadvertently pointed the Sword at them. And as the Book was still sealed, he had no idea what it might contain. Charismatic? I thought he was a prat. And I'm sure he'd speak highly of me too. I've no idea where he is now. In a moment I'll have one look on Facebook, but no more than that. I had very strong 'Keep Away' signals in that respect.

Your Sword and Book was eventually seen by Bob Stewart in the Witchcraft Museum at Boscastle. Not sure if you'd have appreciated that! *Wicca wicca wicca, witch witch witch...* Did the boy-wonder Kevin donate them? I suppose they're still there. Your comment about his appearance: 'This could not possibly have been coincidence by any chance.' Well, I've long since put this sort of thing down to the meaninglessly meaningful stuff that the Universe often throws at us. I may be dreadfully wrong, but I don't think he did anything much with 'your' Sangreal.

Two last letters in the folder and then *Hey Ho! Off we jolly well untangle…*

Alan

Wm. G. Gray
14. Bennington St.
Cheltenham
Glos. GL50 4ED

Telephone

(0242) 24129

10 AUG 1990

Dear Alan, I hear from Marcia today that you (or rather your wife God bless her) have recently had your 3rd daughter on whom may I congratulate you all to which Bobbie adds her good wishes too, By a strange chance I am just going through your latest book, EARTH GOD RISING...

Well first of all it's a well-written book, but I'd expect that from you anyway, though Laura Jennings does scream a bit loudly at the start with all the Osirian stuff, though he <u>was</u> about the earliest recorded "Green Man" and I've seen much of him in Egypt. Though I've only recently seen an article written by Maggie Murray back in 1916 in which she claims that the Holy Grail mythos was of Egyptian and Coptic origins and does a hell of a. lot of far-fetched etymology to back it up, but there was a fashion for that then, like claiming witchcraft meant the work of the wise rather than the work of the wicked, but you know my feelings about that, and oddly enough it was old Doreen Valiente who first put me wise to it.

I'm always arguing with Laura (who's never been to Egypt) about this craze for revalidating Egyptian Gods in modern dress, and I still can't see the point of trying to do so. But I found your claim that Herne derives from the rutting-cry of stags a fascinating theory and most strongly probable though also it signifies the Horned One, and as you noted the horn always signifies the erect penis besides being the means of old-time artificial insemination which I think you might have mentioned. I've seen the Serapeum at Sakkarah and it is indeed quite impressive to this day, possibly where the worship of Mithra started too. Did you know that children who smell the breath of the sacred Apis ox were supposed to be gifted with the knowledge of futurity? Also that if he lived till the appointed time they drowned him in the river Nile and then embalmed his body and entombed it with much ceremony.

Anyway, I liked your book, and I suppose in a way it complements my support of the anima in my Goddess book by validating the animus or "Eternal Male Principle" for its own sake even though we know perfectly well one can never be complete without the other. But think how dull it would be if we fornicated like fish, the female laying the eggs and the male just swimming over the spot shooting sperm in the same direction, Perhaps that was the origin of the saying "Poor Fish". Thank God we're not androgynous - yet!

Marcia tells me that Katherine Kurtz has just been consecrated as a Bishop of the Liberal Catholic Church by a retired Franciscan Bishop? Oh well, I remember little Ernie Butler was a priest of that lot, and he was a dear soul if ever there was one.

But it seems as if you wanted Cernunnos to take the final bite in the persona of Herne. No real reason why it shouldn't, though I don't know if Marcia has told you of her "Herne" (who is a local lad at present being held for grand larceny and is quite convinced that he and he alone is Herne and will destroy the whole world very shortly by the power of his invincible mind. Oh well, whom the Gods would destroy etc)

For some reason I can remember one Midsummer being on a hilltop with a few that Geoffrey Ashe got together to challenge Arthur who was reputed to ride over with the Wild Hunt and some clot would insist on singing "This is Buddah" which I objected to in Britain, I felt that Ashe was a rather nasty little man really.

Anyway I hope my few remarks help sell your book, and am hoping to get something started for the Sangreal in Britain before I go but I very much doubt if anyone here is seriously interested in anything I care about. Anyway I'm told that with regard to the Zodiac murders in New York City (who hasn't been caught yet) that the police are trying to locate all those who have been borrowing from public libraries any books by Crowley "a Black Magician and drug user of evil repute" in the hope of finding their murderer amongst them. Poor old Aliester. I wouldn't have called him Black though he would certainly have been a murky grey. I wonder if he's back yet? He'd be so flattered to think his books were still impressing people, especially to commit murder. I'd hope mine might inspire someone to do some real good amongst his/her folk. I expect yours might do the same, and if this one gets even a few

people out in the open and wondering what might be in them sometimes, who knows where that contact might lead??
KQ and FFFF to you.

Bill

The Atrium   18th April 2023

Hello Bill!
If there's a portion of yourself within me at this moment, then you've just come back from a fierce work-out at the Cardiac Rehab class. I go there once a week. I was quite fearful at first, being pushed to exert and extend myself in case I went too far, but I enjoy it now. I've come straight from there and am hot, sweaty and probably smelly, so I stay a safe distance from anyone else and keep my toxic armpits as sealed as any of Putin's nuclear silos that might soon open and destroy the world. I'm definitely getting stronger and more confident, less afraid. Not yet Rocky III, but enough to start small adventuring with Margaret again.

   I'm feeling two things: pleasure at getting stronger, in company with people who are considerably older than me and who have been through similar; plus a certain melancholy about this correspondence ending, as I can see there is only one more letter to answer.

   'Rutting stags'… Actually I stole that bit from Pat Crowther, so it wasn't a clever insight from me. I've never heard stags so much as snort or fart, never mind bellow during rutting. And I don't think I *did* note that the 'horn always signifies the erect penis.' Did I really write that, or were you slipping yourself into my writerly Self? That sounds like your sort of thing.

   Herne, Cernunnos… As I think I told you, I cleave toward this energy more than any others, but I don't do any Wiccan kind of worship. Nothing outward anyway. The anagram KISS pretty much sums up much of what I do, and how my brain works. *Keep It Simple, Stupid.* Used by the US Army originally. A lot of people think I'm a bit thick, and I'm not about to disabuse them. You see, years ago I had something better and more purposeful than any kind of occult initiation: I learned the non-verbal communication of British Sign Language. This reduces everything to its crucial essence, and made me *think* differently. Not better, you understand, but *differently*. The BSL sign vocabulary and language structure is *very* different to spoken or written English. Minimalist, I suppose.

   I babble. Here in the Atrium, on actual and symbolic levels, toward the end of the working day, I have a sense of you being present for the for the first time.

You seem kind. At peace. Smiling. Chatty but not bossy.

And while I note the usual KQ – Keep Questing, I also raised an eyebrow at your FFFF. I think you're being a bit cheeky here, because I know that this was used by the British Army to mean *Find 'Em, Feel 'em, Fuck 'em and Forget 'em.*

Bless you Bill,

Alan

HWTL as we say.

15 JAN 1991

Dear Alan

Bobbie and I are both very sorry to her of your father's death at that precise moment. Not so much the actual death, because we all have to do that but at all the problems it must have caused you. Is your mother still alive? I wish it could have been me instead. What bothers me is the rapidity of reincarnation these days. My wretched mother scarcely had any time out at all, and DF only had eight years. And if we're all just one person anyway, what does it matter in the end? Seems to me they've scarcely got your corpse in the oven than you're swimming for dear life up someone's vaginal canal. I do hope your father gets kinder treatment than that. I've actually met a man who remembers being born.

    Or rather the nightmare he kept having of a pair of hands reaching for him with the shirt-cuffs turned back and a pair of cufflinks dangling from them. One night when he was about nine, the nightmare was especially vivid and he woke up screaming. His mother came rushing in and he told her. Then she nearly passed out and told him the story. The hands were those of the doctor who'd delivered him. She had him at home and the doctor had arrived late and only just had time to whip off his jacket, loosen the cuffs and gran the baby as it popped out. When he realised the hands were trying to help, not hurt him, he never had that nightmare again.

    My own mother remembers being an old sick woman dying in Paris, and a nurse came in. She tried to say: "Who sent you? I can't afford a nurse" and all she could manage were a sort or gurgles, so she thought: "My god I must have had a stroke, I can't even speak." When she noticed the nurse was lifting her up she tried to say "I'm too heavy for you put me down." And then she noticed a baby and tried to say "What are you doing with that child, this is no place for a baby. Take it away at once." But again there came nothing but a gurgles, and the nurse seemed to be speaking a foreign language and the baby appeared to lifted up and down. Then she realised to her horror that the baby was <u>herself</u> in a mirror and she must have died and got reborn in another country (it was the USA). Suspecting she was Noemie Cadiot, I was able to place her death…

Kevin has Jacobus' book at the moment, but IF I can get it back, will you promise to read through it and LET ME HAVE IT BACK PLEASE!! There's a few flaws in it and I've written no fewer than four letters not one of which has he answered, so I've written Jacobus out altogether.

My walking is terrible and co-ordination very bad now. It's a much as I can do to get to the Post Office for my pension these days. Forgive my not writing any more, but this is about as much as I can do. My writing days are definitely over, so carry on the good work.

And God be with your father's soul…

KQ

Bill

Garden Office   Mam's birthday. April.

Dear Bill,

In your very last letter to me, with the ribbon of your typewriter clearly almost dried up, you honoured my Dad. I suppose the symbolism of that is what brings a lump to my throat.

He was pretty much a useless Dad, as I often thought in my youth. He was irritating and annoying when I could bring myself to speak to him with all the contempt of my Inner Pharaoh. I think I've told you that already, but the thing is I think of him every day. He spent the whole of his working life from 14 onward as a coal miner, and never escaped. Barely literate, as racist as the rest of his generation, he never saw a 'real live Black man' until he was 60, and then only in passing. My Mam, the great Dark Mother who damaged my childhood, described him as 'the most ignorantest man she'd ivver met.' I can look back now at many incidents and take her point, but...

If your friend remembers being born, I remember choosing them both as parents in that timeless time Between Lives. So I shouldn't have whinged or played the martyr or done any humble-bragging about how poor we were.

Yet now I'm nearly 72, with increasing intimations of my own mortality, I wish I could do some Quantum Time-travelling and go back to give Dad in particular some kindness. As he said to me once, via a medium in Glastonbury, 'I'm sorry son...I did my best.'

I wrote a whole book about him that you might have liked, if only because of the military background - *Geordie's War.* Possibly the one book I'd choose as my 'best'. It was ostensibly about his War Hero father (i.e. my grandfather whom I never met). It was really about a different sort of War: between me and my Dad; between him and *his* Dad. And probably between every Father/Son relationship since the patriarchies began a million years ago.

Dad was hopeless, daft, and I miss him dreadfully. I ache to make amends for the things that I'm only now, at Dad's own age, beginning to understand. And that, increasingly, goes for my Mam too. There would have been secret wars between them that I would never have known about.

Perhaps this might be the case with your 'spiritual son' Jacobus? I think he's still alive, as he had some contact recently with David Conway. I've no desire to connect.

I suppose that in a differing way you've been a sort of Dad to me over many years. I'm feeling guilty about some of the onslaughts I've made against you in the preceding letters, but isn't that what sons do? I've never thought of it like that before.

So...

I suppose the Garden Office is as good a place to end this as any. It's bright, with a fine westerly breeze. There's a glider, very high and far, glinting as it catches the sun. I've just hung the washing out on a line and made a right balls-up of it. I'd like to say that the birds are all flocking around in a sort of pathetic fallacy, but there's no sign of them. I won't take it personally now, though.

Although, even as I write that, I can see that the blackbird we call Meatloaf and the two magpies have *just* appeared as if on cue, so I'll take this as a good omen to finish on.

For all your faults – real or imagined – you were a true Scatterer of Light for generations completely unaware of your impact.

Bye Bill – and Bobbie!

Bless you both

Alan

HWTL

DISENTANGLING

After any formal, magickal ritual, you should close everything on outer and inner levels and earth. I saw Basil, after a hefty rite at Hawkwood, stand in silence for a moment doing whatever inward stuff was necessary and then he simply touched the ground with one hand. Almost like a benediction.

I suppose I'm now doing similar with this book. I don't need to do any formal 'banishing' of those mighty souls who have floated through my psyche for the past few months, although as I write this I can hear the sound of distant sirens that always make me think of Banshees. So maybe I've upset someone 'up there/out there/in there' (they're all the same place) - or else They're coming to get me.

So what happened after Bill's final letter?

By many accounts he and Marcia had a spectacular falling out and he decided that she wasn't DF reborn after all. Whatever she may have thought herself, Marcia never once mentioned this to me, though I've no doubt she felt DF's overshadowing – is it innershadowing? I think all of us have felt that energy at some time, in some way, and wondered for a Timeless nano-second whether *we* were DF reborn. She comes and then she goes, like the magpies cavorting in our garden now. And I've just this very moment received an amiable post from Marty via Facebook on unrelated topics! He doesn't know I'm doing this, and I've no desire to ask him what really happened. I don't want or need to know. (I sound like Bill Gray now!)

I also heard that Bill completely cast aside his quondam 'spiritual son', as mentioned in his very last letter to me - though I've no doubt that Jacobus himself might dispute that and get his hundreds of Sangreal members to barrack me. I actually had to trim down Bill's letters to cut down on his endless spleen toward those who he felt betrayed or failed him. I realise that Bill, like me, struggled with forgiveness, and I've no doubt that in due course he would have fallen out with me too.

I've no idea whether the Sangreal Sodality has survived in any shape or form anywhere, other than the small, private Temple that Marcus tells me he maintains. Perhaps it is like the tiny shoots in the garden that I can see from the window... with water, sun, nourishment and love it might grow and thrive. But I still maintain that, as Bill defined it, *his* vision of the Sangreal is not relevant in today's multi-racial, multi-dimensional consciousness.

So *I* touch the floor now to earth whatever is floating around, and give a knowing wink to the two magpies outside.

Good day and God speed and Go well to all who stumble upon on this book...

HWTL

Alan Richardson

Unedited extract from Aleister Crowley's unpublished diary of 1922. As given to me by William Gray, who probably got it from Gerald Yorke...

*** I am myself a physical coward, but I have exposed myself to every form of disease, accident, and violence. I am dainty and delicate, but l have driven myself to delight in being dirty and debauched, disgusting, and to devour human excrements and human flesh. I am at the moment defying the power of drugs to divert my destiny and disturb my body from its duty. I am also a mental and moral weakling whose boyhood training was so horrible that its result was that my will wholly left my mind an animal soul like an elephant in the rut broken out of self. A morality more severe than any other in this world if only by its freedom from any code of conduct ***

I love my love with an L because she is lustful, and I lent her a lot of lira because I am trustful. I took her out to lunch at Lafayettes, lentil soup, lobster and lettuce, and then on to lemon ices, lychees and limburger, because she looked such a lanky lengthy slimburger. I looked for liquor all through the liberal list and bought her Liebfraumilch and Lachryma Christi, Lafitte, and London Gin and Chateau Leonville, because I wanted to keep her out of the way of ill. I gave her a lump of lard because she was lean, and a little lewd lyric I learned in a latrine, because she likes to listen to Lohengrin, And then I let Lucille loose making her clothes, some lingerie too because her linen was loathesome. She laid in lavender loose and laced because her legs would wander up to her waist. I gave her larkspur, laburnum, lobelia and lily, to wear in her hair because she looks so silly. And many a like device I did as well, to prove how much I love my love with an L, "With an L?" she said with rudeness, "but L stands first for Lewdness." Then for lechery lust and laughter, with lascivious leers sent after. Love me with the lance that pushes, proudly through your bristly bushes, with the leaping of the lion that in vain one keeps an eye on. With a lordliness that begs no ones leave to part my legs. With the tight and wrinkled lump, that keeps banging on my rump, Love me with the L of looking for the aftermath of cooking. With a liking for the wine sold in this old shop of mine. And the steaming plat de jour that my kitchen tolls procure. Love me with the L of longing, still unsated by the thronging tireless triumphs of our joy, with the first love of a boy. Mad with that last lust that hollows their huge horror of the gallows. Love me with the L of lordship over language, that by wardship of my worship from fatality winning poets immortality. Love me with the L of lashing lust to know much tortured thrashing writhing madness that all time may not match in filth or crime. Also love me with the L of light above me shining from your stainless soul that always had its God for goal. Gain him by the dissolution the illusion of pollution. Love me with the L of lips that I bite until blood drips down my thirsty throat and grips next between my harlot hips while your tongue obscenely slips into sleekest sin or dips darkly over us its death and whips lust with his twisted finger-tips to perverse pleasures that eclipse fertilities frail fallow hips. But also with such lips that swore to track down truth forevermore. The poisonous pulp, the rotten core, the bitter rind, the seeds designed to multiply their evil kind. Love me with the lips that curled and smiled their challenge to the world and sang so stern so smooth so strong, so subtle and sublime a song that Hell made holiday for Pan to have taken on the flesh of man. Love me with lips more curved than Keats, where foulness coos and beauty bleats. With lips more passionate than Shelley that suck all night a whores raw belly, With lips that tempting Shakespears kiss boast sodomy and syphilis. Lips that drip white with sailors spunk across the smeared shit of his punk, yet by her soul her cunt outstunk. With those lips love me soaked in slime, let them more subtle and sublime in eloquence most high and holy, majestic and yet melancholy, yet should their inspiration falter, find grace free flowing at my altar. Love me with an L for licking lewd leased lows of longitude for lapping these leaks and loving to suck all holes too small for shoving. O love me an L your Leah because I let my leucorrehoa loose like a lady a young river to irrigate your lazy liver. O love me with an L for lending my life, my love, my unpretending and modest mouth, my mild melodious empurpled arsehole, my commodius old cunt, winking at you from the front. My nipples, navel, ears and nose, all else I have is wholly yours you rotten doped dirty dog to get you hot on. What do you fancy your next stunt'll be? Where your prick is, you bet my cunt'll be. O love your love with one more L boy, because her lungs might be to hell boy. And yet she only breathes to fashion forms for the pleasures of your passion. O fuck my cunt O stuff my dung O cook me with your cock and tongue. O piss and shit with me and vomit, then make witches dinner from it. Sauced with such other dirt as your whores carrion may squirt. O see my cunt whose outer seam is grimed with grisly red and green. Gay gonorrehoa with stinking smears of verdigrised urine. Orange bleared of blood and cakes of shit over this, my bum bruised azure, mauve, and indigoed point of piss. I crave you prick with all the might of an insane Boanerges rogering a rainbow. O frig my arse, O tongue my twat, O chew my menses, sniff my snot, O grease my gob with greasy grot. O make our joy a juicy job. We wont be bound by fancy sweaters, We'll teach young L to know his betters and love with all the other letters.

I love my Leah with an A, because her. arse goes all the way.
I love her with a B because, a better bottom never was.
I love her with a C for newer, was cunt so crazy or so clever.
I love her with a D for main I dote on her dung divinely dainty.
I love her with an E, my pen trails so far less eager than her entrails.
I love her with an F, embrace, her frigging fingers, her fucked face.
I love her with a G for gripping her guts to save my prick from slipping.
I love her with an H, I relish her hole because its heat is hellish.
I love her with an I, her mission is intestinal intuition.
I love her with a J, I am a judge of jelly-juice, her jam.
I love her with a K, I think she has a kick in every kink,
I love her with an L, for weeks, I lie and lick her where she leaks.
I love her with an M, I fuck, her mouth her menses and her muck,
I love her with an N who thought I could be nasty and so naughty.
I love her with an O, refusing, no offal from her ovaries oozing,
I love her with a P, my bliss is to be her pisspot when she pisses.
I love her with a Q, I swim in the quintessence of her quim.
I love her with an R, I've gotten a red raw rump, rich ripe and rotten.
I love her with an S shes IT, with spunk slime slobber, snot and shit.
I love her with a T, shes got my tool tucked tight in her tarts twat.
I love her with a U, she hands me a uterus that understands me.
I love her with V, no swine are so velvet vile as her vagina.
I love her with a W, my whore, with whom I have a willing war,
I love my Leah with an X, the unknown quantity of SEX,

I love her with a Z, I'll pack her zigzags by Zeus with my great Zacker. I wish instead of twenty six letters to love her, I had pricks!

**** I will not go on with this damned thing, I am more certain than ever that cocaine is no good under any conditions at all unless in very small doses and very few of them. This prolongs the agony and turns me into a dull prolix word-cobbler.

**** Dreamed that I had been made pope by some illegal means, I was afraid of being found out by my ignorance of routine. My chaplain, who had put the deal over I fancy, couldnt be found when I needed him to coach me.

Feb 12, 1922. This is the last will and testament of me, Edward Alexander Crowley. I give and bequeath the whole of my property to Leah Hersig of New York USA and Cefalu Italy. I appoint her my sole executrix.

       Edward Alexander Crowley.

**** I've been talking to Leah about my sexual life and comparing certain recent troubles with my refusal to climb the Alps after having been to Chogo Rhee. It is an essential part of my character and indeed the master-key to my whole career that I simply cannot do anything, however easy in appearance, which does not promise an achievement beyond anything I have ever attained before. Hence the tragedy of Hilarion broke my heart. Alostrael succeeded in mending it at last, and then the Gods smashed it by killing our babies. Their idea was doubtless to 'prevent me from being distracted from my work as Logos, The result in any case has been to disenchant me with sex altogether, I cant even take any interest in it. Oh well, the outcome of it all is with Them.

(**L** was Crowleys private code for ejaculation)

Printed in Great Britain
by Amazon